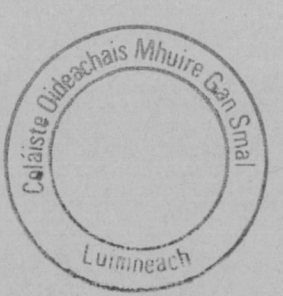

MUNSTER
RUGBY GIANTS

HUGH FARRELLY was born in Cork in 1972 and grew up in Saudi Arabia before returning to Cork with his family in 1979. Educated at Presentation Brothers College and UCC, he took up rugby at the age of eleven and went on to play for Munster schools, Munster u20s and the Irish Universities. After leaving UCC with a Commerce degree in 1994, he joined Lansdowne RFC in Dublin and worked with AIB for a year. Returning to Cork in 1995, he took up employment with Irish Pensions Trust (IPT) and joined Dolphin RFC. In 1997 he was on the Dolphin team, coached by Declan Kidney, that won promotion to Division One of the All-Ireland League for the first time in the club's history. Hugh gave up his job with IPT in 1997 to study journalism at Coláiste Stiofán Naofa in Cork, and began working for the *Irish Examiner* in August 1998. He currently works as a sub-editor and sports columnist for the *Irish Examiner* and is still playing senior club rugby with Dolphin.

MUNSTER RUGBY GIANTS

The Rise and Rise of Munster Rugby

Hugh Farrelly
with a foreword by Tom Kiernan

THE O'BRIEN PRESS
DUBLIN

First published 2001 by The O'Brien Press Ltd,
20 Victoria Road, Dublin 6, Ireland.
Tel: +353 1 4923333; Fax: +353 1 4922777
E-mail: books@obrien.ie
Website: www.obrien.ie

ISBN: 0-86278-728-9

British Library Cataloguing-in-Publication Data
A catalogue record for this title is available from the British Library

1 2 3 4 5 6 7 8 9 10
01 02 03 04 05 06 07 08 09 10

The O'Brien Press receives assistance from

the arts
council
an chomhairle
ealaíon
50ᵗ

Editing: The O'Brien Press Ltd
Layout and design: Designit
Colour separations: C&A Print Services Ltd
Printing: Zure S.A.

PICTURE CREDITS

All photographs courtesy of the *Irish Examiner*. The publisher and author would like to thank *Irish Examiner*
photographers Kieran Clancy, Des Barry, Dan Linehan, Richard Mills, Norma Cuddihy and Denis Minihane.

CONTENTS

DEDICATION

This book is dedicated to Jill and me Mam, my two favourite broads, for their unwavering support, and also to the mighty men of Munster for always giving us something to get excited about.

ACKNOWLEDGEMENTS

I would like to thank everyone at The O'Brien Press, in particular Rachel Pierce for all her help and patience in editing this book, and also Caitríona Magner, Tony Sutton, Michael O'Brien and Íde ní Laoghaire. Special thanks to Frank Murphy for his wonderful work in designing the book.

Thanks also to Jim Coughlan, Peter Walsh and John Cramer at the *Irish Examiner* for their assistance with the pictures, and to Tony Leen for being so supportive of this venture.

Many thanks to Tom Kiernan for being so helpful with the foreword, and finally to Declan Kidney for finding time in his busy schedule to talk to an old pupil.

PASSING THE TORCH TOM KIERNAN

It is a privilege and a pleasure to be invited by Hugh Farrelly to write a foreword to this book on Munster rugby, particularly as it records the province's progress since the game went open in 1995. The recent successes the team has enjoyed in Europe have created an enormous interest in and enthusiasm for the game in the province, whilst at the same time gaining the respect of new opponents and spectators throughout the European rugby world.

There are many who would say that this respect has been earned down through the years by the province's performances against the major rugby touring countries. I can vividly recall watching, as a child, the heroic performances against the Australians in Cork in 1948 and against South Africa in Limerick in 1951, when highly controversial refereeing decisions in the dying moments of each game deprived Munster of victory. Since then, however, great success has been achieved against both Australia and New Zealand. Although success for the province against South Africa is yet to come, the South African scalp was taken in Limerick in 1965 by the Irish Universities, captained by the legendary Munster and Irish centre Jerry Walsh.

The present group of management and players seem determined to maintain this respect and tradition. The essential ingredients of a successful team are not the sole preserve of Munster, but the present group does possess a huge work ethic, an ambition to maximise their talents and a positive attitude to overcoming adversity rather than dwelling in self-pity or disappointment.

This attitude, of course, is largely due to the skills of the management team and coaches. Declan Kidney and Niall O'Donovan, together with the highly respected and knowledgeable captain Michael Galwey, constitute a formidable force. Their achievements against opposition teams with far greater resources have been enormous, yet they have always maintained a great sense of realism and know that there is only the width of a post between success and defeat; Saracens and Northampton spring to mind. Furthermore, they have achieved a marvellous rapport with and respect for their wonderful supporters, who have gained a reputation for their sportsmanship and knowledge throughout the rugby playing fields of Europe.

It is against this background that Munster can look forward to the future. There are huge challenges ahead, but with the continued support of the Union, the Branch, the players and spectators, I believe the province can indeed look forward with confidence.

Ireland's captain, Tom Kiernan, shakes hands with Eamon de Valera, president of Ireland, at the Ireland v. Scotland game at Lansdowne Road in February 1968.

HE SOUTH

Munster captain *Terry Kingston (centre) clenches his fist after his team was awarded a penalty try during the epic win over Australia at Musgrave Park in 1992. Sharing Kingston's exultation are Mick Galwey and Peter Clohessy (left), and Paul McCarthy and Richard Costelloe (right).*

Munster rugby has always been special. The game as played in the province has a quality that quite simply sets it apart from the rest of the island – a fact that has been reflected in a string of famous victories over the years. The most famous remains the unforgettable 1978 defeat of the mighty All-Blacks, a fearsome team that was largely unacquainted with the word 'lose'. But lose they did, and Munster remains the only team in Irish rugby to have ever administered that bitter pill.

However, even by those standards, the seasons 1999/2000 and 2000/2001 stand out as a truly remarkable period in the history of Munster rugby. Although the ultimate goal of the European Cup has not yet been attained, this team, under the masterly control of Declan

When the chips are down, *Munster supporters come out in force. Three-year-old Ciaran from Limerick sports his team's colours at Thomond Park during Munster's win over Saracens in 2000.*

Kidney, has captured the public's imagination in a way that has revolutionised Irish rugby. Once almost exclusively the preserve of the upper middle class, the game has now started to move beyond the cities and is beginning to rival GAA as the sporting passion of rural Ireland, and a great deal of this has to be attributed to the success of Munster. Their ability to claw back from seemingly inevitable defeat, to stay focused and composed under pressure and to enjoy every game with unparalleled spirit and verve has endeared them to fans not only at home but around the world. In short, their performances over the past few years have been nothing less than inspired and inspiring.

The most famous of their recent victories was undoubtedly the stunning European semi-final triumph over Toulouse. Fans who were present on that sunny afternoon in Bordeaux puff out their chests like war veterans when they recall the events of that momentous day. But there were other days too, like the cold January afternoon in Thomond Park when a last-gasp Keith Wood try and a Ronan O'Gara conversion saw off the marauding Saracens. And the equally cold night a year later at Rodney Parade when Munster conceded fifteen points in the first-quarter, only to roar back in the second-half and defeat Newport in a manner that left the home support bewildered and confused.

These displays came from a tremendous inner belief and a never-say-die attitude, which together created a force greater than the sum of its parts. Pundits could not fathom, and indeed some still cannot, how star-studded English Premiership sides could be defeated by a host of relative unknowns. Of course, that made victory even sweeter!

It has been a remarkable journey in just a few short years. It started when Declan Kidney took over in 1997, and between then and now Munster and their fans, the irrepressible Monsters, have enjoyed a rollercoaster ride through domestic and European rugby. Along the way stars have been born. Young men such as Ronan O'Gara, John Hayes, David Wallace and Peter Stringer, previously unheralded, have become major sporting celebrities, while existing icons, such as Michael Galwey and Peter Clohessy, are now *bona fide* Irish rugby legends, mentioned in the same breath as Willie John McBride, Tony O'Reilly and Moss Keane.

The Munster trio of Donal Spring, Les White and Moss Keane get stuck into the All-Blacks during their famous 12-0 victory at Thomond Park in 1978.

One of the secrets of Munster's success is the fact that it is a true provincial team: it draws on players from every county in the province, all playing with such commitment, skill and passion that they have won over legions of fans province-wide. Previously, unless a major touring nation was being entertained, provincial games would attract only a few hundred die-hard supporters, but such was the extent of the Munster phenomenon that Musgrave Park in Cork and Thomond Park in Limerick attracted thousands of fans for mere warm-up games against Leinster and a Rest of Ireland selection respectively. Mick Galwey, in particular, has been a huge influence, and not just through his leadership on the field. The Kerryman's GAA background has struck a chord with Gaelic fans who might never have picked up an oval ball in anger, but are now much in evidence on Munster away trips. Likewise, the emergence of Clanwilliam's Alan Quinlan as a player of international quality has made him a celebrity in his home county, Tipperary, and has done wonders for the game of rugby in an area that has long been staunch hurling country.

The support of the fans has been essential to the ascent of the Munster star. It is the visibility of their support that is important: where once Manchester United and Liverpool jerseys abounded, children now proudly parade the red jersey of Munster and imagine they are Ronan O'Gara or Mick Galwey when playing ball in the back garden. And when the fans take to the stands in stadiums, the Red Tide washes over the opposition in a wave of noise, enthusiasm and pride.

But what is it that sets Munster apart? For answers we must look to the historical and sociological aspects of the current phenomenon.

Historical precedent is important: the current Munster side draws a huge amount of inspiration from the great deeds of the past. In 1905, Munster became the first province to face a major touring side. Although they went down 33-0 to the mighty New Zealanders, they nonetheless started a tradition of Munster Might taking on the full force of foreign challengers. Touring sides soon learnt that the men in red *never* give up.

In 1967, after a succession of near-misses, a Munster side, captained by Noel Murphy, became the first Irish province to defeat a major touring team when they beat

Australia 11-8 at Musgrave Park. Then, in 1972, only a penalty goal in injury time foiled Munster as New Zealand fled from Musgrave Park with a 3-3 draw. Revenge is a dish best served cold, they say, and Munster were to wait six years before serving it up in style.

The auspicious date was 31 October 1978 – it remains the greatest day in Munster history, and one of the proudest in the annals of Irish rugby. Graham Mourie's New Zealand team had embarked on a tour of Ireland and Britain with a star-studded squad that had achieved a

Munster hooker *Pa Whelan celebrates Cantillon's try as the bewildered All-Blacks embark on an unfamiliar journey ... behind their own posts.*

comprehensive victory over the Lions a year earlier. They were considered unbeatable, but given Munster's record against touring sides and their narrow escape from Musgrave Park six years previously, the All-Blacks were taking no chances. They selected a side full of established Test players for the game in Thomond Park. The All-Blacks won every other game on that tour, including all their Test matches, but that afternoon in Limerick they never stood a chance.

Mighty deeds were done that day. Seamus Dennison's bone-crunching tackle on Stu Wilson set the scene. Then there was Tony Ward's immaculate kicking, the strong running of Jimmy Bowen, and Christy Cantillon scorching over for the only try of the game, all now part of Munster rugby folklore. A famous story from that day concerns the one and only Moss Keane, who packed down in second-row with Anthony Foley's father, Brendan. Munster was ahead 12-0 with only minutes left on the clock. Andy Haden, the giant 6ft 6ins New Zealand lock, frustrated by the way events were unfolding, clenched his fist, ready to throw a punch. Big Moss wrapped one of his huge mits around Haden's fist and, looking him straight in the eye, said, 'Don't bother, ye'll only lose that as well.' Realising that the battle was lost, Haden obligingly backed down.

Munster were not done with touring sides. In 1981 Tony Ward played a blinder at Musgrave Park as the Australians, who went on to beat Ireland in the Test, went down 15-6. Munster's reputation as a minefield for tourists

Jimmy Bowen pins back his ears and sets off on the run that led to Christy Cantillon's try against New Zealand in 1978.

MIKE MULLINS

BORN: 29/10/1970

When Mike Mullins moved to Munster it was a spiritual homecoming for the New Zealander. The IRFU had been trawling the globe looking for Ireland-qualified players, especially backs, and their investigations had thrown up the names of Australian Matt Mostyn and Mullins. At the time, Mullins could have been placed under the banner of 'journeyman professional'. He had been plying his trade with the less-than-illustrious West Hartlepool club in England, and it was after a difficult season there that he decided to make a move. He had offers from France to consider, but thankfully he decided to move to Limerick and join Young Munster.

A key factor in this decision was Mullins's father, for although Mike had been brought up in New Zealand, where he had represented the All-Blacks at u21 level, his dad, Thomas, hails from Limerick, and Mullins discovered relations strewn liberally throughout the area.

He admits that the circumstances which brought himself and fellow import Mostyn to Ireland put them under enormous pressure to perform, given that they were taking the places of home-grown players. It was pressure Mostyn couldn't handle, and he left Ireland for Newport in Wales after a poor season with Connacht and a few cheap caps for Ireland. But with Mullins it was a different story. His family links meant he had a greater affinity with the area, and he threw himself heart and soul into his new venture.

Picked for the Ireland A side in 1999, Mullins was selected on the squad to tour Australia that summer, and though he did not play in either Test, he won his first cap against Argentina later that year. The emergence of Brian O'Driscoll has meant that further caps come only when the Leinster genius is unavailable, but Mullins has never let his country down and he has probably been Munster's most creative player over the same period.

A strong tackler and good passer, Mullins also has great speed off the mark and the ability to run at angles that take him away from defenders. Never was this better demonstrated than when he came off the bench against Newport (he was recovering from a broken jaw) and ran in a wonderful try from fully forty metres out – not unlike O'Driscoll's wonder try for the Lions later that year.

The Munster experience has affected Mullins deeply, as he puts it: 'We have something special, and I'm not sure that we know exactly what it is. We all get on, the team, the guys on the bench, the guys who don't even make the bench, no one wants to let their friends down.'

was cemented in 1992, once more against the Aussies at Musgrave Park. That was a truly remarkable victory. Australia were the reigning World Champions, a professional outfit in everything but name; their opponents played together approximately four times a season. Bob Dwyer, the Australian coach, foolishly underestimated Munster and chose to rest some of his key Test players. Even so, on paper, it looked like no contest. But the home side, superbly led by Terry Kingston, simply refused to be beaten.

The mass brawl that broke out between Munster and Australia led to the dismissal of Mick Galwey and Garrick Morgan at Musgrave Park in 1992. It may not have been pretty, but it showed Munster's refusal to be intimidated by the World Champions.

__Munster full-back__ Charlie Haly, who kicked vital points that afternoon, is mobbed by the delirious crowd at Musgrave Park after the win over Australia in 1992.

It was a hot-tempered encounter, with the smaller Munstermen choosing to take on their exalted opponents in a tough physical battle. A mass brawl saw Mick Galwey and his Australian second-row counterpart, Garrick Morgan, sent off. The key score of the game was the penalty try awarded to the home side after a succession of scrums on the Australian line. Then, with the teams tied at 19-19 and the game nearly over, young Brian Walsh launched a massive clearance kick downfield. From the resultant line-out, Ben Cronin soared highest and scrum-half Derek Tobin's pass found substitute out-half Jim Galvin. His superb drop-goal sent Musgrave Park into raptures and earned Munster another famous victory.

This brave, proud tradition has been absorbed by the current squad, helped by the presence of Peter Clohessy and Mick Galwey who both played that afternoon against Australia. However, when Declan Kidney took over as coach he was determined that Munster, while respecting and taking inspiration from the heroes of the past, would make their own mark on Irish and world rugby. One could safely say he has succeeded.

Bitter rivals PBC and CBC clash in the Munster Senior Schools Cup in 1998. The two Cork schools have provided a regular production line for Munster and Ireland over the years.

The Limerick rugby nurseries of St Munchin's and Crescent College, seen here in the Munster Schools Senior Cup in 1999, are to Limerick what Pres. and Christians are to Cork.

Kidney's success is due to his skill as a coach, but it is also due to the calibre of player he has at his disposal. That calibre originates in the passionate love of rugby that defines the southern counties and the style of rugby taught and played there. There has always been a special quality about the rugby played in the province, and undoubtedly a great deal of this is rooted in the Limerick–Cork factor. Unlike Leinster, Connacht and Ulster – where the game has traditionally revolved around one large urban centre – Munster has always been split between Cork and Limerick. In the past, this has created its share of difficulties. The inter-city rivalry sometimes meant that getting picked for the province could well depend on how many selectors hailed from your neck of the woods. However, the two cities tend to produce different breeds of player, and the best Munster sides have always successfully merged the two styles.

Over the years the Munster squad has combined tough, gritty forwards from Limerick, men such as Tom Clifford, Brendan Foley and Colm Tucker, with skilful backs from Cork, such as Tom Kiernan, Michael Kiernan, Moss Finn and

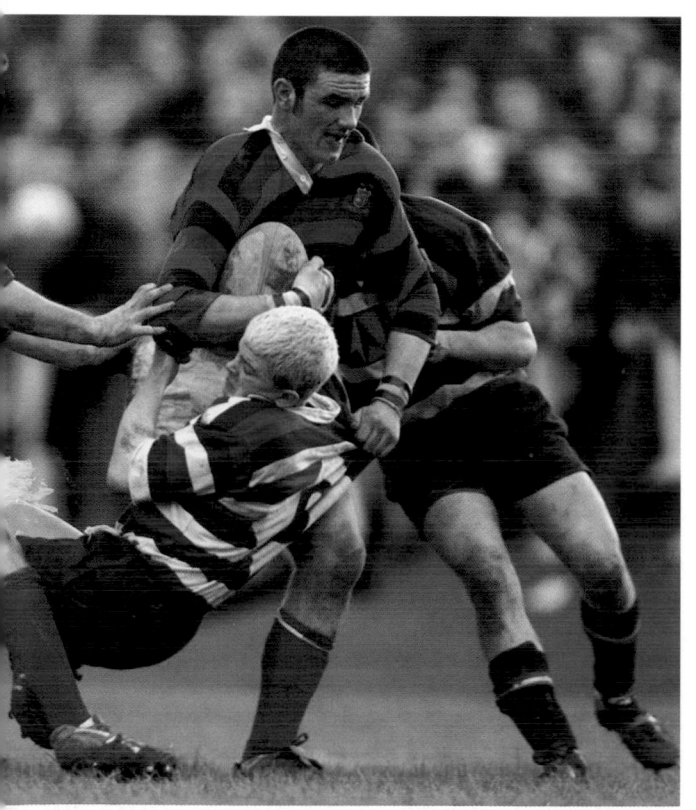

Ralph Keyes. Stereotyping? Perhaps. There were, of course, famous backs who played their rugby in Limerick – Seamus Dennison, Philip Danaher and Garryowen's adopted son Tony Ward, to name a few. There were also many great forwards born and bred in Cork, for example, Noel Murphy, Donal Lenihan and Terry Kingston. Nonetheless, there is a hardness about Limerick rugby that lends itself to the production of teak-tough forwards, whereas the internationals who graduate from Cork's clubs generally tend to ply their trade in the backline. Recent history backs this up. Clohessy, Wood, Hayes, Galwey, Foley, Quinlan, Halvey and Wallace are all superb forwards for Munster and all learned their rugby in Limerick. Then we have Stringer, O'Gara, Horgan, Kelly, O'Neill and Crotty in the backline, who all cut their rugby teeth by the banks of the Lee.

The differences in playing style stem from the different backgrounds in each city. Traditionally, rugby in Cork has followed conventional lines. The game was mainly confined to private secondary schools, notably the famed nurseries of Presentation Brothers College (PBC) and Christian Brothers College (CBC), which meant rugby was always a middle-class sport in the city, as it is in Dublin and Belfast. There is an old Cork joke about the wealthy woman from Montenotte standing on St Patrick's Bridge yelling, 'Help! Help! My son the doctor is drowning!' Well, her son was more than likely educated in Pres. and UCC and played rugby for Cork Constitution.

The situation in Limerick could not be more different. The city has its own rugby nurseries in St Munchin's and Crescent College, but, as is the case in Wales and New Zealand, rugby in Limerick is completely classless. Doctor and docker pack down side by side, and the city remains the only place in Ireland where the oval game is more popular than either GAA or soccer. It might be denied loudly within the confines of Dublin 4, but there is absolutely no doubt that Limerick is the spiritual home of Irish rugby.

There has always been a desire in Munster to put one over on Dublin. Cork and Limerick share a strong identity with their province and a determination to prove that rugby in Ireland is not centred around Lansdowne Road and Donnybrook. Over the years the spoils have been shared in the annual clash between Leinster and Munster in the Interprovincial Championship, with Munster pulling slightly ahead since

the late 1990s. But the introduction of the All-Ireland League (AIL) in the 1990/1991 season provided the perfect opportunity for the southern clubs to make their point. Cork Constitution won the inaugural title, and since then Munster clubs have shared it between them, until St Mary's from Dublin – the only team to consistently challenge the Munster sides – deservedly broke the sequence in 2000. There is no doubt that this run of club victories strengthened the sense of identity for Munster players, which in turn had a strong impact on the provincial team. Although club rivalry within the province is intense, it is always far preferable for another Munster club to win the title than a side from Leinster, Ulster or Connacht. This attitude can be summed up in two words: Munster Pride.

Munster clubs have dominated the All-Ireland League since it began in 1990/1991, until St Mary's of Dublin won the title in 2000. Second-row Steve Jameson (above) secures possession against Young Munster at Tom Clifford Park in 1998.

Shannon's Dara Kirby wins line-out possession ahead of Young Munster's Denis O'Meara during another hotly contested Limerick derby at Tom Clifford Park in 1999.

PETER CLOHESSY
BORN: 22/3/1966

Prop forward Peter Clohessy, like his long-time friend and colleague Mick Galwey, has achieved cult status in Munster and Irish rugby circles. He has had a colourful career, to say the least, which reached its highest point when he managed to reinvent himself as a loosehead and play a starring role for Munster and Ireland in the twilight of his career, and its lowest point when he was suspended for stamping on French second-row Olivier Roumat in 1996.

Clohessy had established himself with Munster long before his call-up to the national side. He has now played for the province in three separate decades. He was alongside Galwey on the Munster side that beat Australia in 1992, earning the wrath of Australia's outspoken coach, Bob Dwyer, in the process. However, any ill-feeling Down Under towards the Claw had obviously dissipated by the time Queensland offered him a one-year contract in the late 1990s, and he acquitted himself very well during his spell in the Southern Hemisphere. Apart from that season with Queensland, the Claw has been a dedicated member of the Young Munster club, contributing to the most memorable day in their history, when they captured the All-Ireland League title in 1993.

Noted as a disruptive scrummager, Clohessy won his first Irish cap against France in 1993, and was unlucky not to make the Lions tour that summer, especially when it became clear the players chosen ahead of him were simply not up to the task. Except for the World Cup in 1995 – when he was unavailable due to work commitments – the Claw was first-choice Irish tight-head until the unfortunate Roumatgate affair. That incident allowed Paul Wallace into the number three shirt and, at the age of thirty, many predicted Clohessy's international days were at an end.

Following his suspension, the Claw was cast into the international wilderness, and it was during this period that he tried his luck Down Under. Despite his international exile, the Lions still selected him for the tour to South Africa in 1997 but, cruelly, injury ruled him out and, once again, Paul Wallace stepped into the breach.

Then came his reinvention. The Irish side that faced Georgia in the World Cup qualifier in late 1998 once again had PM Clohessy on the team-sheet, but this time at loosehead. The switch to the left-hand side of the front-row meant less onerous scrummaging duties and allowed him more energy to pop up around the field. By now fully subscribed to the lifestyle of the professional, the Claw subsequently played the best rugby of his career for province and country. His performances during Munster's assault on Europe were immense, and he was no less effective at international level. Clohessy's special place in the hearts of Munster fans was evidenced by their chant of 'Who let the Claw out?' during the clash with Newport at Rodney Parade.

As well as supplying the required steel in the set-pieces, Clohessy has surprised many with his abilities in the loose. Unfortunately, when it came to the 2001 Lions selection for Australia, he missed out for the third tour in succession. His age counted against him, but considering the scrummaging problems encountered in the second and third Tests, one cannot help but wonder if the result would have been different had the Lions bared their Claw against the Aussies.

Even though the ultimate honour for a British and Irish player has eluded him, Peter Clohessy will be remembered as one of Munster's and Ireland's finest.

A drenched but delighted Declan Kidney
revels in Munster's victory over Colomiers
at Musgrave Park in December 1999.

THE

CHAPTER TWO

DRILL SERGEANT

I'm just part of the wheel,'
says Kidney, 'and we're trying
keep that wheel going for as
long as we can.'

Munster has been fortunate with its coaches over the decades. The team has been coached and managed by a succession of devoted men who worked as hard as their players to achieve their goals. In 1997 a new man sat into the driving seat. Declan Kidney has proven a dynamic force, pushing the team to ever greater achievements and steering them expertly into the twenty-first century. His quiet, constant belief in his players is the cornerstone on which their success has been built. He is fearless when it comes to creating goals and envisioning the future. As his number two Niall O'Donovan said prior to the final at Twickenham: 'We set goals at the start of the season, and one of them was to win the European Cup.' If those same goals had been voiced at the beginning of the 1999/2000 season, the response would most likely have been incredulous mirth. That Munster were to fail ultimately by a single point was tragic, but it testified to the belief within the squad and its management team that they could achieve what many would have regarded as the impossible.

To understand the development of this Munster side, it is first necessary to understand Declan Kidney, the reluctant hero of this story. Considering the awe with which he is now regarded, it is strange to think that Kidney got the job by default. In 1997, as was and is the trend, the Munster Branch was seeking a high-profile, overseas coach to take on the job. First, they went after Welshman John Bevan, and then Kiwi Andy Leslie who already had experience of coaching in Ireland. While Leslie hummed and hawed, Kidney was asked to help out along with O'Donovan. It was a stop-gap measure and one that must have damaged his pride, surely? 'No, not at all,' replies Kidney, 'it was an honour to be asked to coach the provincial team no matter what the circumstances. I knew if I did a good job I would be kept on, and that's what happened.'

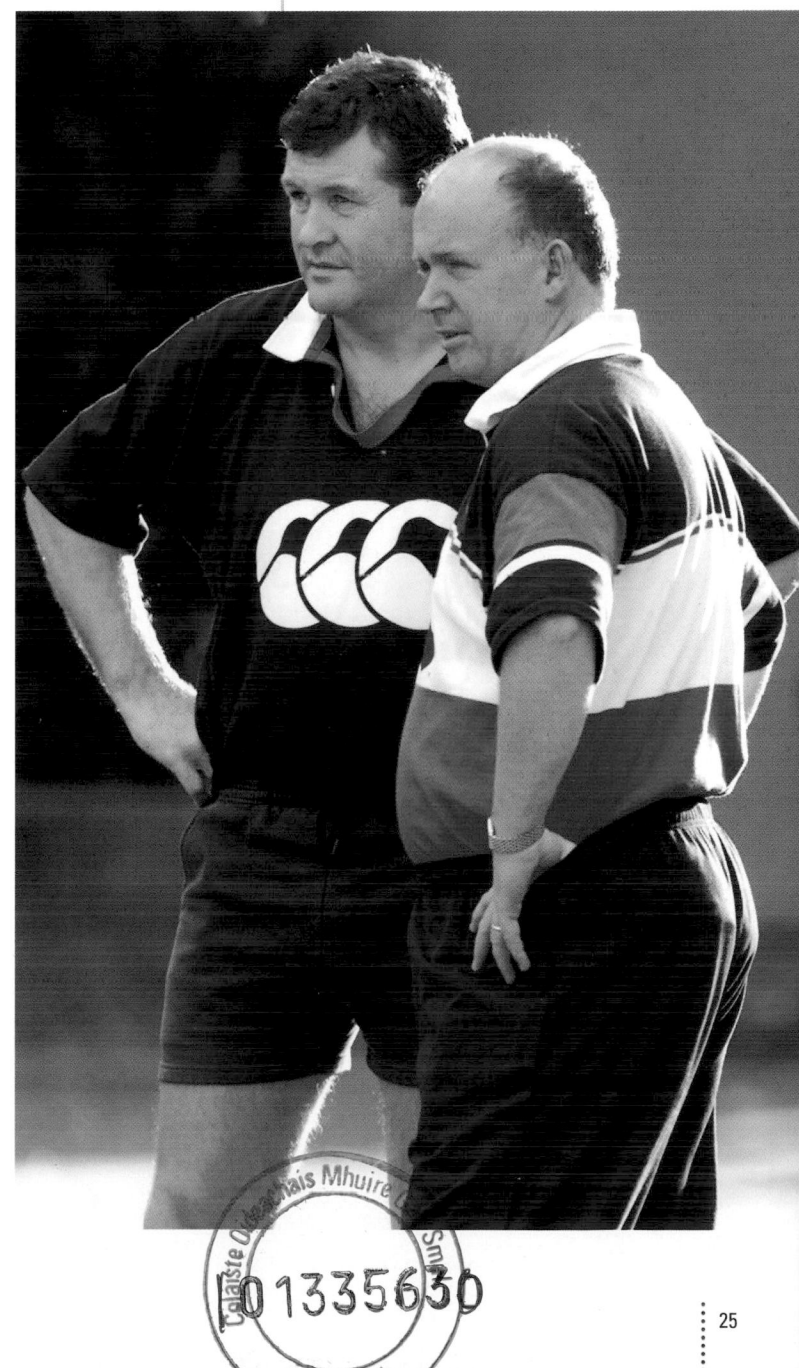

Niall O'Donovan's assistance has been crucial to Kidney and Munster. 'I'm lucky that I have Niall beside me,' says Kidney. 'If I'm getting too intense he taps me on the shoulder and I tone it down.'

Maths teacher and rugby coach at PBC, Kidney returned to university to study to become a careers guidance officer, and though he did go on to change a lot of careers, it was not in the way he had originally envisaged. Throughout his life, rugby has been his first love. He was a highly successful rugby coach at schools level. Together with his sidekick, former referee Paddy Attridge, he led PBC to four Junior Cups in a row and then to four out of five Senior Cups. This success was followed by his appointment as Irish schools coach, and he was in charge when they toured New Zealand in 1992.

In 1995 Kidney was installed as coach of his old club, Dolphin RFC, where, during his own playing career, he had proven himself a competent outside-half. He stated boldly that it was his intention to get Dolphin into Division One of the All-Ireland League within three years. His first season there was difficult to say the least, and the Musgrave Park outfit would have been relegated were it not for a last-minute change to the rules by the Irish Rugby Football Union (IRFU). The following season, with largely the same squad, he steered Dolphin to promotion a year ahead of schedule. The only two games the team lost occurred while Kidney was away with the Irish u19s in Argentina. It was arguably his greatest coaching achievement up to that time, and it ensured his name cropped up when Munster needed help in the autumn of 1997.

By the time season 1999/2000 came around, the groundwork had been done. Kidney had a solid management team in place, a team he knew he could

Brian O'Brien, who went on to manage the national side, threw himself heart and soul into his role as Munster manager. Here he leads the squad in a chorus of 'Stand up and Fight' following the win over Saracens at Thomond Park in January 2000.

The spirit within the Munster camp is legendary, as prop John Hayes testifies: 'The craic we have together has a lot to do with our success.'

depend on. Both assistant coach Niall O'Donovan and team manager Brian O'Brien were proud Shannonmen and, more importantly, they were Munster to the very core.

Niall O'Donovan played for years as number eight for Shannon, and he won four Munster Senior Cup medals with the club. He was a strong, abrasive player, good enough to play interprovincial rugby for his province. Then, as coach, he guided Shannon to four consecutive All-Ireland League titles. Munster and rugby were in O'Donovan's blood. His late father, Jim O'Donovan, had been second-row on the Shannon team that won the Munster Senior Cup for the first time in 1960. Apparently, fresh from victory and after numerous renditions of the Shannon anthem 'There is an Isle', Jim wanted to name his new-born son after one of his cup-winning team-mates. His wife, however, was having none of it. She preferred to name the boy Niall after one of her relatives. The story goes that Jim thought about it for a while and then relented. 'After all', he pointed out, 'there is a Niall!'

Declan Kidney selected an uncapped Peter Stringer over internationals Tom Tierney and Brian O'Meara, forcing O'Meara to switch to Leinster. Here, O'Meara gets the ball away under pressure from Stringer during a clash between Leinster and his old province.

Brian O'Brien played centre for Shannon in the 1960s and gained three caps for Ireland in 1968. When his playing career ended he became a successful administrator and a hugely respected figure in Munster rugby circles. Crucially, he, like O'Donovan, had the respect of the squad and was entirely committed to the cause. John Langford tells the story that when he met O'Brien in London for the first time, the Munster manager ignored the Australian's proffered hand, moved close to him and pinched his stomach, checking for excess body fat. This kind of single-mindedness is common to Kidney, O'Donovan and O'Brien – they were the Holy Trinity of Munster rugby.

JASON HOLLAND
BORN: 12/8/1972

When Jason Holland fielded a phone call in New Zealand from his good friend Damon Urlich, little did he know what effect it would have on his life. Urlich was player-coach with Midleton RFC, a small club with big ambitions, located half an hour from Cork City. They were looking for an out-half to help their assault on the All-Ireland League. Holland agreed to help out and, though injury meant he didn't turn out for the East Cork club as often as he would have liked, he was instrumental in guiding the junior club into the second division of the AIL.

Although it was his mesmerising form at out-half that made him a hero at Midleton, Munster coach Declan Kidney was quick to spot an opportunity. Kidney knew Holland's rugby pedigree was sound – he had played thirty-five times for Taranaki in New Zealand – and after watching him perform wonders for Midleton, he invited him to join the Munster squad for their assault on Europe in 1999/2000.

Ronan O'Gara had the Munster number ten jersey firmly in his possession, so Kidney decided to employ 'Dutchy' at inside-centre. The highly accomplished Killian Keane had been first choice for several seasons, but Horgan managed to displace him, and the Munster midfield of O'Gara, Holland and Mullins quickly became one of the most potent in the game. A first-centre with the hands and kicking ability of an out-half is of immense benefit to O'Gara, who knows that if he has to ship on the ball under pressure, Holland has the ability to launch a booming clearance downfield or execute a long miss-pass to split the opposition's defences wide open. And perhaps most critically, Holland is a punishing tackler, not content to merely bring his man down, he likes to use his power to drive him backwards.

Despite having a centre of Allan Bateman's ability, Northampton got no change out of the Munster midfield that day at Twickenham, and Holland showed his all-round ability with a perfectly executed drop-goal. Happy with his life in Munster, the residency rule means Holland can represent his adopted country. If called on, he will no doubt prove to be as valuable an asset to the green jersey as he has been to the red.

By 1999/2000, Kidney had also earned the respect and admiration of his players, although he admits that, at the start, his methods took a while to catch on. His coaching style had undoubtedly been influenced by his schoolteacher background and by the fact that the majority of his experience was at underage level. For old hands like Peter Clohessy and Mick Galwey, the renowned Kidney mind-games were a little hard to adjust to. 'There were teething problems,' concedes Kidney, 'but there always is when a new coach takes over. I am lucky that I have had Niall [O'Donovan] beside me. If I'm getting too intense he taps me on the shoulder and I tone it down.' Over his first two seasons in charge there was a little give on both sides, and now there is nothing the players would not do for their coach.

Mick Galwey *goes over for a try against Ulster during the Northerners' European Cup-winning season of 1998/1999. Ulster's European success was an inspiration to Kidney's side. Note the empty terraces at Musgrave Park – it was the season before the hype really got going.*

Munster scorched to the *Interprovincial Championship in 1999/2000. Shannon and Munster team-mates Eddie Halvey and Alan Quinlan celebrate their win over Connacht at Thomond Park.*

Throughout his coaching career, from PBC juniors right up to Munster, Kidney has listed out goals for the season, and on every occasion top of the list has always been: 'Enjoy yourselves'. But this is not just token coach-speak, Kidney actually means it. In an era when the primary motivation for a lot of modern sports professionals seems to be money, Kidney's squad is characterised by their spirit of enjoyment. 'They are people first and players second,' he says. 'Our primary objective is that we enjoy ourselves.'

Mick O'Driscoll claims a good line-out ball against Ulster in 1998. The talented young second-row has learned from the guile and experience of John Langford.

A lot of the credit must go to Kidney and his backroom team for creating the right kind of environment. Mountainous prop John Hayes explains it: 'The spirit is the major factor. We all just love playing together. The *craic* we have together has a lot to do with our success. When the chips are down on the field, that comes through. We just want to play for each other.' Munster training sessions are not a safe place to be if you are a sensitive soul as the slagging is unrelenting and merciless. The players seem to genuinely enjoy each other's company, and at crucial stages in important matches this willingness to do their utmost for their team-mates has been invaluable to Munster. That desire to do the best by their fellow players continues off-field too, but not because Kidney forcibly instils it. Unlike most other coaches, he does not impose an alcohol ban between matches, instead he trusts his players. 'They are all professionals, they know what they can and cannot do for themselves, what will affect them and what won't. It's left up to them.'

If there is one quality that defines Munster's coach it is his modesty: 'I'm just part of the wheel,' he says, 'and we're trying to keep that wheel going for as long as we can.' We are not dealing with a Bob Dwyer figure here, a coach whose every utterance is dominated by his own ego. Rather than seek the limelight, Kidney positively shrinks from it, preferring to point to the supporting roles of others when success is lauded. 'As Director of coaching you employ all these different people and I'd like to think that if I have done anything right, it was to bring these guys on board.'

Of course, these unassuming qualities have further endeared him to players and supporters alike, but, as the saying goes, everybody loves a winner, and the most influential factor in Kidney's popularity is the success he has brought to the province.

While the spirit described by Hayes has been crucial, games are not won simply because of the desire to win. Kidney's innovative coaching methods and methodical preparation have been instrumental in Munster's successes during his tenure. His coaching style encompasses many different elements. It is a considered approach, intelligently tailored to suit his squad, their abilities and their limitations. He explains the thinking behind his approach: 'We look at four angles in getting a team ready: fitness, skills, psychological readiness and the social aspect.' Psychological readiness means taking out the element of surprise. Though Kidney regularly trots out the 'we're just worrying about our own game' line for the media, the opposition is, in fact, exhaustively analysed and examined for weaknesses – when Kidney sends his players onto the pitch they are well briefed and are very rarely deceived by their opponents.

A keen student of psychology, Kidney has been known to read from psychology books in team meetings in a bid to motivate his troops. While deliberately keeping a certain distance from his players socially (the best coaches are never one of the lads), he takes a deep interest in each player's personal life in order to have each man in the best possible frame of mind on the field. On one occasion, while he was coaching Dolphin, he demanded that the club help a young outside-half find a job because 'how could he be expected to make crucial decisions on Saturdays if he wasn't making any during the week?' Kidney adopted the same approach with Munster, firmly believing that a happy squad is a successful squad. The overseas players in the Munster squad – John Langford, Mike Mullins and Jason Holland – have all been taken care of to ensure that their off-field experiences are as happy as their on-field ones. Kidney's mind-doctoring has been highly successful, he has managed to keep such talented players as Frankie Sheahan, Mick O'Driscoll, Donncha O'Callaghan, Killian Keane and Tom Tierney committed to the cause even while they were forced to wait in the wings.

One of Kidney's greatest skills is his ability to spot potential early and to select players who complement each other's strengths and weaknesses: the hallmark of a gifted coach. He sees it as a distinct advantage that the majority of the team hail from within the province. 'The pack that played in Twickenham consisted of seven Munstermen and one Australian,' Kidney points out. 'In building the team I first look at Munster players, then Irish players, then Irish qualified players and finally overseas players who I think can help younger members of the squad with their experience.'

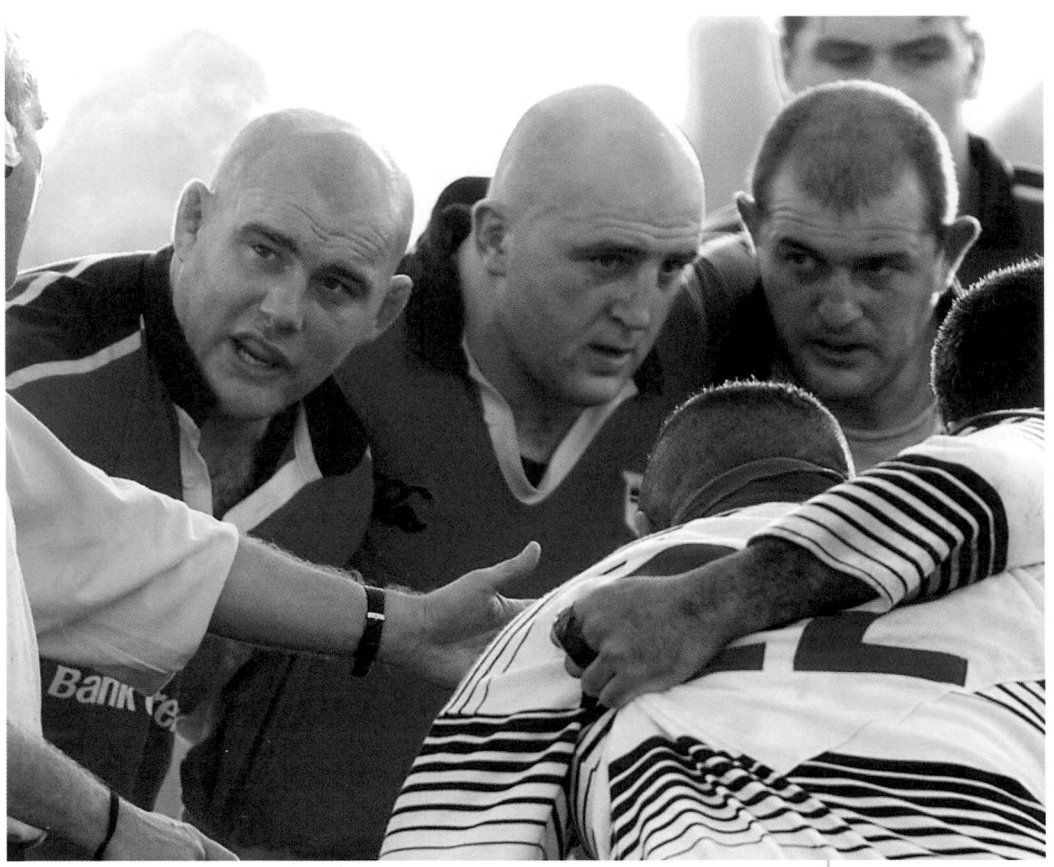

His unexpected selection of Eddie Halvey, an amateur at the time, against Stade Français in the European Cup quarter-final was inspired. Halvey's athletic leaping at the front of the line frustrated the French line-out and gave Munster a significant advantage. Kidney sees things others don't. When he started selecting the slight student Peter Stringer over the more robust and experienced Tom Tierney and Brian O'Meara, it raised a few eyebrows and eventually led to O'Meara's transfer to Leinster. However, in young Stringer's laser-like passing, Kidney recognised an ingredient that could contribute greatly to his backline's potency. He also realised that anything the Corkman lacked in physical presence was more than made up for by his bravery and desire to win. And just as Kidney's visionary qualities elevated Stringer to a scrum-half of international quality, his consistent selection of Anthony Horgan and John Kelly – two players not widely rated beforehand – saw that pair blossom and prove their detractors wrong.

Keith Wood's arrival from Harlequins provided Munster with a world-class hooker and an inspirational leader. The front-row combination of Hayes, Wood and Clohessy was one to be feared throughout Europe.

In the professional environment, where players are expected to train daily with the same faces, it is easy to become stale, but the Munster backroom team has managed to keep training schedules fresh and innovative. For each big game Kidney finds different ways of motivating his players. John Langford gives his assessment: 'Declan Kidney is a great coach and a great man-manager and always comes up with something new. You have to admire the way he can place a different type of emphasis on every match.'

So Kidney proved he had the qualities of a winning coach, but how far could he take his team? At home, the Interprovincial Championship separates the wheat from the chaff. In season 1998/1999 there were signs of greater consistency. The format of the championship had been changed to a double programme of matches, allowing each team to meet twice. This new approach was a huge success. The quality of rugby was good and the matches drew large attendances. The climax came at Donnybrook on 23 October 1998 when Munster defeated Leinster, in front of their own fans, to take the title.

However, conquering Europe was the main objective. The province's record had been unremarkable since the competition began in 1995/1996. For the first three years they failed to get beyond the pool stages and had never won an away game. There had been some notable victories in that time, however, especially over English giants Wasps and Harlequins, both at Thomond Park.

In the 1998/1999 European Cup, Munster came out of a group containing Perpignan, Neath and Padova, after recording their first ever away win in the competition when they beat Padova 35-21. The Italians were far from being the strongest side in the draw, but the victory was very important psychologically. 'When we played Padova in the last group game in 1998, we had already qualified and people said it didn't matter,' says Kidney. 'But I thought it was hugely significant in that it was our first win away from home. That gave us confidence because we knew we *could* win away from home.' However, in the quarter-final, a trip to France proved less productive as eventual finalists Colomiers disposed of Munster 23-9. It may have been a sound defeat, but it served to strengthen resolve within the ranks for the following season. Young players, such as the UCC duo Peter Stringer and Mick O'Driscoll, emerged from that thrashing older and wiser.

There was a general belief that Munster could not win in France – a problem common to all Irish teams at that time. Over the years, trips to France had yielded nothing but a succession of defeats as Castres, Toulouse, Bourgoin, Perpignan and then Colomiers lined up to dole out the pain. Kidney knew that he would have to organise resistance to the French if Europe were to be conquered. Meanwhile, the Munstermen could only gaze on enviously as Ulster convincingly beat three French sides on their way to the European title. Packed

houses at Ravenhill witnessed thrilling wins over Toulouse and Stade Français before Munster's conquerors, Colomiers, were sent packing at Lansdowne Road in the final. Undoubtedly, home advantage, and the fact that the English clubs were not involved, was of immense benefit to Ulster, but it nevertheless proved that it could be done. It banished the inferiority complex Irish teams had been labouring under as a result of regular defeats in the international arena.

Ulster's coach, Harry Williams, had developed a simple game-plan. He had a competitive pack to provide possession, an uncompromising defence, an experienced out-half, David Humphreys, pulling the strings, and Simon Mason at full-back was one of the best goal-kickers around. It may not have been hugely exciting, but it was a recipe for success. Kidney knew that he had a more rounded squad at his disposal and that with a few key additions, Munster would have a side that could emulate Ulster's achievement – even with the English teams back on board. 'The Ulster victory meant an awful lot,' says Kidney. 'Ulster showed the way.'

The summer of 1999 was very productive. Keith Wood's return from Harlequins was a huge boost. For various reasons, Wood had never really developed a relationship with the province, and had been vocal in the past about his indifference to the red jersey. He had been on the Harlequins side that was defeated at Thomond Park two seasons previously, shortly after he had made those ill-judged comments. Suffice to say, he wasn't the most popular man in Thomond that day. The story has it that as Harlequins were running out onto the pitch the announcer, in a bid to be hospitable, exhorted the crowd to 'give Keith Wood a real Limerick welcome'. There was a stony silence, then some wag shouted out, 'Stab him!'

True or not, two seasons later Wood was welcomed back to Munster with open arms and he threw himself wholeheartedly into the enterprise. It was hard luck on Frankie Sheahan who had done his time and was ready to become the first choice. Sheahan contemplated leaving the team as a result but, to his eternal credit, on Kidney's urging he decided to stay. 'Keith himself came up to me and said, "Look, it's like this. We can work together as I am only here for the year, and I will give you all the help I can and hopefully I can learn from you as well." I have learned so much from him and he has picked up the odd thing from me, too,' admits Sheahan.

Munster not only gained a world-class player in Wood, they also had a man who knew how to motivate those around him by word and deed. This guy was a genuine star, and even the unflappable Kidney seemed slightly daunted: 'What am I going to tell Keith Wood after he has been with the Lions and Jim Telfer?' he wondered. The arrangement turned out to be of huge benefit to Wood, too, who was rejuvenated by his spell away from the unrelenting, congested season in England.

If Wood's arrival was important, then so too was the signing of the giant Australian second-row John Langford. Mick O'Driscoll had been successfully blooded over the previous two seasons but was still very young and a little raw. Langford, by comparison, brought vast experience with him, as he had represented Australia four times and made numerous appearances for ACT Brumbies. And with Mick Galwey by his side, it meant Munster had a battle-hardened engine room and two players who complemented each other perfectly. Signing Langford was also an investment for the future because the youngsters, Mick O'Driscoll and Donncha O'Callaghan, could not but benefit from having a player of Langford's ability to draw on.

Mike Mullins's relocation to Limerick had provided Ireland, and Munster, with a top-quality centre. Another New Zealander was called into the Munster squad in the shape of Jason Holland. He had played many times for Taranaki and had been brought to Ireland by his long-time friend Damon Urlich, player-coach at Midleton RFC. Despite missing a large part of the season due to injury, Holland had been a huge success in East Cork, helping to guide the club from the Munster Junior League into the Third Division of the AIL. He was seen originally as back-up to Killian Keane, but he would go on to play a far more influential role for the team.

The line-up was now in place, so it was time for Munster to fall in and show what they were made of. The pre-season jaunt took the squad to Wales, where a friendly against Dunvant had been arranged.

Considering that it was only July, the match was a well-contested affair that the visitors duly won on a 26-21 scoreline. The first round of the Interprovincial Championship was played at Cork Constitution's ground at Temple Hill (due to the unavailability of Musgrave Park and Thomond Park), and Leinster were beaten comfortably 31-20. The match was notable for Ronan O'Gara's first try for his province and John Langford's début appearance on home soil. Following this, Connacht were demolished 67-17, a scoreline that few expected and that demonstrated the try-scoring potential at Munster's disposal.

Then came the big test: a clash with the European champions, Ulster, up north. Over the years, Munster had found it well nigh impossible to win in Ulster, so their performance there would be a good barometer by which to gauge their readiness for their away assignments in the European Cup. The subsequent 25-24 victory was a huge psychological boost for the squad, proving to the players that they had what it would take to inherit Ulster's European mantle.

Meanwhile, the Irish squad was preparing for the World Cup and had, rather foolishly, agreed to a warm-up fixture against the Munstermen in Musgrave Park. This turned out to be a day of loyalties. There was no doubt where the crowd's allegiance lay as the thousands present roared on the men in red all afternoon. However, the fact that the Munster players in the Ireland squad (Wood and Clohessy) had leaked the line-out calls was rather more unexpected, and resulted in Mick Galwey and John Langford having a field-day out of touch. It was a special day for Galwey. He had been deemed not good enough to play for Ireland, despite playing the best rugby of his career, so to lead his province to an unexpected victory against the national side was particularly sweet for the big man from Currow.

The Interprovincial title was wrapped up with three more wins, all of them convincing. Ulster went down 36-19, Leinster 30-13 and Connacht were whipped again, 53-10. Morale in the Munster camp was extremely high and the training sessions were a happy place to be, with the players totally confident in their backroom team and in each other. It was very much a case of 'Roll on Europe'.

JOHN LANGFORD

BORN: 26/6/1968

Declan Kidney needed a foil for his captain, Mick Galwey, in the Munster second-row and his choice of John Langford proved to be inspired. The wily Australian was over thirty years of age when he signed, but was in superb physical shape and brought with him a wealth of experience, which he has passed on to promising youngsters Mick O'Driscoll and Donncha O'Callaghan. Langford had appeared for ACT Brumbies on sixty-five occasions, and had won four caps with the Wallabies in the mid-1990s. Were it not for the presence of a certain John Eales in the Australian engine room, he might well have added considerably to that total for the two were very similar in build and style.

A wonderful athlete, Langford's 6ft 7ins frame, prodigious leap and secure hands make him a guaranteed ball-winner in the middle of the Munster line-out and at restarts. He is also a huge threat on the opposition throw and pilfers many a valuable ball for his side. However, Langford is much more than just a means of securing possession and frequently pops up around the pitch to take on the ball, which is never turned over. In contrast to some of the Southern Hemisphere mercenaries who come to Europe at the tail-end of their careers solely to earn easy money, Langford is an integral part of the spirit of this Munster team and also of his club, Shannon. The minute he stepped off the plane at Shannon Airport, he says, he was made feel welcome and he speaks warmly of his time with Munster as the happiest in his long career. The picture of an emotional Langford arm-in-arm with his coach, Declan Kidney, after what he thought was his final match for Munster in Lille, spoke volumes.

Langford travelled back to Australia in the summer of 2001 to watch the Lions tour and try to secure a professional contract. However, unable to find suitable employment with one of

Australia's Super 12 sides, he was only too happy to take up Declan Kidney's offer of a third straight season with Munster. A factor in his decision was Munster's acquisition of his friend and former ACT team-mate, Jim Williams, who, ironically, had joined the province on Langford's recommendation. But it wasn't a tough decision – the second-row knew he was returning to an environment that suited his rugby and his family and, of course, there was one other small matter: 'I have unfinished business with Munster regarding the European Cup,' said Langford on his return ... too right.

GATHERING MOM

ENTUM

CHAPTER THREE

Colomiers, Pontypridd, Saracens: these were the teams that stood between Munster and the knock-out stages of the European Cup in 1999/2000, and they were a daunting challenge.

Colomiers were the beaten finalist and the team that had ejected Munster from the competition the previous season. They had a tough, rugged set of forwards and, like all French teams, flair and invention out wide. Whereas Munster could be reasonably confident of victory at home, the province's dire record on the continent meant the trip to France was a huge psychological hurdle that would have to be cleared if they were to have any hope in the competition.

Then there was Pontypridd, experienced campaigners in Europe – although they had lost the services of point-scoring machine Neil Jenkins. They had an astute coach in former Wales flanker Richie Collins and some promising young players, like their second-row Ian Gough, ranged alongside experienced performers, such as Dale McIntosh.

Finally, Saracens: the glamour boys from London and the scalp that would yield the greatest satisfaction. Consistent success on the international stage had led the English to develop a conviction that rugby in their country was superior to that played anywhere else in the Northern Hemisphere. This was fuelled by the huge money and hype of the Sky TV-promoted Premiership League, which had fostered a condescending attitude towards the rugby played in Ireland, Scotland and Wales. Only the French teams were treated with anything approaching respect. The English media smugly wallowed in the belief that the absence of their teams in 1998/1999 had totally devalued the European Cup, rendering Ulster's victory quaint but

ultimately meaningless. Saracens typified the modern, money-driven English club side. They had amassed a host of international stars, all attracted to London by the promise of high-living and hard cash. As well as their South African player-coach, World Cup-winning captain Francois Pienaar, they had French ace Thierry Lacroix, Aussie flyer Ryan Constable, Europe's most promising second-row Scott Murray and, to cap it all, could also call on English Lions Richard Hill and Tony Diprose, as well as Lion-in-waiting Danny Grewcock. A formidable array of talent backed by a supreme self-confidence.

Munster certainly had their work cut out for them. Given the difficulty of their group, it was no surprise when they were quoted at odds of 50-1 for the trophy, with one English bookmaker even listing them at 66-1. The general consensus was that the winners would almost certainly come from England or France, and the Irish sides were simply not rated as serious contenders.

Munster kicked off their campaign at home to Pontypridd and, without setting the world alight, managed to run out comfortable winners at Thomond Park on a 32-10 scoreline. There was a decent crowd present that day, but nothing exceptional, with plenty of space around the ground. After a blistering start, there were elements for Declan Kidney and Niall O'Donovan to work on as Pontypridd were allowed back into the game, but overall it was hard to argue with the final scoreline. Mike Mullins played at full-back, and while he did some good things in attack, the feeling was that he would have been better utilised in the centre. Anthony Foley was man of the match and Ronan O'Gara kicked well, but the performance as a whole was more workmanlike than inspirational. But that was encouraging in itself – that a team doing so well in Wales could be dismissed so clinically. However, the win did not create many ripples in the competition and the bookmakers failed to see any reason to greatly alter their initial appraisal of Kidney's men – especially with Saracens next up at Vicarage Road. It was marked down as a banker home win, and in the days before the game Kidney built up the opposition

expertly. 'We are not travelling just to make up the numbers,' he said, 'but they are a top-class outfit. They have a huge number of top-quality players, but that's why we're competing in Europe, to take on the best.' Perfect! The 'we're just happy to be here' line was guaranteed to induce complacency in the opposition.

Munster did have some vociferous support at Vicarage Road, but the Monsters were heavily outnumbered by the fez-wearing Sarries. At half-time Munster trailed 21-9, and with nine minutes to go they were behind 34-23. It didn't look like their day. Referee Didier Mene had done them few favours – he disallowed what Keith Wood claimed was a perfectly good try. All in all, it looked as though a brave performance by Munster would end in honourable defeat. What followed was, in Wood's words, 'sheer unadulterated guts' as Munster fought back with tries from Foley and Jeremy Staunton, and an eleventh-hour kick by O'Gara to snatch a one-point win from the jaws of defeat. In injury time, Saracens still had a chance to win it when they were awarded a scrum with a drop-goal definitely on. However, their much-vaunted forwards, as Wood delightedly recounted, were 'hosed off' the ball and a famous victory was banked – one that testified to the dogged belief and determination of the squad. This time the bookies noticed, and slashed the Munstermen's odds to 33-1.

Next up was the dreaded trip to France, scene of so much pain for the team in the past. Injuries meant that Jason Holland came in for Killian Keane in the centre and Marcus Horan took over from Peter Clohessy. There were only a couple of hundred visiting fans in the crowd of 6,000, but they were privileged to witness a tremendous performance by the men in red that day. Colomiers were swept away. John Langford denied them possession, stealing six of their line-out throws; Munster simply would not let them play. Holland and Horan both had excellent games and the visitors were in no way flattered by the 31-15 final scoreline. It was an incalculable psychological boost for the team, burying any sense of inferiority that might still have existed: French sides were now fair game. Yet, typically, Kidney refused to get carried away. 'We would be a dangerous side if we played for eighty minutes,' he opined afterwards. Nothing too over the top there, then.

John Langford looks for support
against Pontypridd at Thomond Park.

On a truly horrible day at
Musgrave Park, Keith Wood tries
to dry his hands before throwing
into a line-out against Colomiers.

Munster wing-forward
David Wallace feels the full force
of De Guisti's tackle in the game
against Colomiers at Musgrave
Park just before Christmas 1999.

'Up for the ba': *John Langford goes up in the line-out against Colomiers.*

The following week Colomiers travelled to Cork to try and redress the balance. It was the week before Christmas, but there was little festive cheer for the Frenchmen at Musgrave Park. It was a truly rancid afternoon with icy rain bucketing down throughout, but Munster showed that, for all their new-found flash, they could mullock with the best of them when called upon. Despite the horrendous conditions, the growing hype surrounding the team ensured that the stadium was packed solid to witness another victory. Keith Wood turned in a man of the match performance, bagging two tries, and the game also heralded the return of Dominic Crotty who came off the bench to score the clinching try. Colomiers were beaten 23-5, and French humour was decidedly not improved by the failure of the showers in the clubhouse afterwards. Coach Jean-Philippe Cariat was rather bemused by the whole Musgrave Park experience. 'It was a funny weekend, really old-fashioned. The stadium, the weather, the changing rooms ... it was like a trip into the past.' From Munster's perspective, the past had never looked rosier, and Kidney could tuck contentedly into his Christmas turkey having secured maximum points from four outings.

JOHN HAYES

BORN: 2/11/1973

Standing 6ft 4ins and weighing in around twenty stone, John 'The Bull' Hayes is by far the most imposing figure amidst a physically well-built Munster squad. The genial farmer from Cappamore in County Limerick has been an essential part of the Munster and Irish teams over the past two seasons, and could consider himself extremely unfortunate not to have made the Lions squad to tour Australia.

Hayes played mainly hurling in his childhood. He made his rugby début at the age of nineteen as a slightly bewildered blindside flanker for Bruff in a 0-0 draw with local rivals Newcastlewest. He has come a long way since that day, and his rugby education was enhanced immeasurably by two seasons spent with the Maorist club in New Zealand. The Bull returned heavier, stronger and more streetwise after proving his worth in that tough environment.

On his return he made the switch from second-row to prop-forward and began to get noticed as part of the all-conquering Shannon sides of the mid- to late 1990s. Hayes was a surprise inclusion in the Ireland squad that toured South Africa in 1998, but he showed the promise there that Gatland would bring to fruition two years later.

Hayes quickly became a regular on the Munster side under Declan Kidney, and he won his first cap for Ireland against Scotland in 2000 when the experienced Paul Wallace, hero of the Lions tour in 1997, was sensationally dropped. His tall frame has led to criticism of his scrummaging prowess, but the fact remains: Munster could not have won so many vital matches if Hayes were an inadequate scrummager. However, there is so much more to his game. Hayes demonstrates a

wonderful capacity for hard toil. His tackle count is up there with the back-row men, while his long arms make him a dream lifter for line-out jumpers. Furthermore, when The Bull hits a ruck or maul, the opposition knows all about it.

Hayes's best day in a Munster jersey came in Bordeaux against Toulouse when he capped a wondrous performance by scoring a memorable try. He was lying prone on the ground during a sweeping Munster move, but he picked himself up, rejoined the fray and displayed a surprising burst of speed to crash over for a vital score.

The Bull's striking appearance and nickname mask a gentle personality, and this, allied to his startling exploits on the field, has earned him something of a cult status in Munster. Cappamore is extremely proud of the big man, and for important Munster games and Irish internationals a 'Good Luck, John Hayes' banner is draped across the width of the village's main street.

Munster spirits aren't dampened by the weather as David Wallace, John O'Neill, Peter Stringer, Tom Tierney and Dominic Crotty celebrate the win over Colomiers.

Mick Galwey enjoys close support from Keith Wood as he goes over for the first try against Saracens at Thomond Park in January 2000.

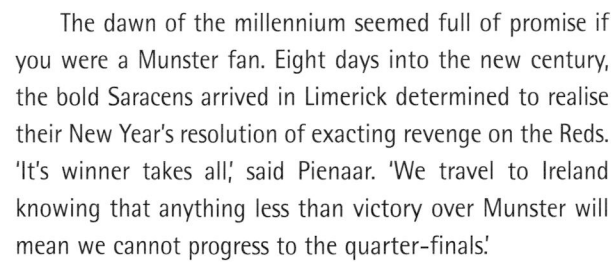

The dawn of the millennium seemed full of promise if you were a Munster fan. Eight days into the new century, the bold Saracens arrived in Limerick determined to realise their New Year's resolution of exacting revenge on the Reds. 'It's winner takes all,' said Pienaar. 'We travel to Ireland knowing that anything less than victory over Munster will mean we cannot progress to the quarter-finals.'

What an occasion! Thomond Park resembled Calcutta train station at rush hour as the two top teams in the group battled for the right to progress to the knock-out stages. The game swung back and forth, but in the first-half it was the English who were stronger as they finished 17-8 in front. Their big guns, Pienaar, Hill and Lacroix, had been in impressive form and the portents were not good. The second-half saw Munster battle their way back into it, but when Sarries' Mark Mapletoft went over for his second try in the 76th minute to leave the score at 30-24, we thought the game was up. It didn't help that one of the Saracens' try-scorers was Cork's own Darragh O'Mahoney, or that another Munsterman, Paul Wallace, had come off the

bench to help kill off his erstwhile team-mates. A few faithless souls were even spotted heading for the exits in order to beat the after-match exodus. But they failed to take into account the remarkable spirit now residing within the hearts of these giants in red.

Munster worked their way into the corner, and somehow Wood managed to tunnel his way over. With the score now 30-29, that left O'Gara with the biggest kick of his career. He lined it up from out on the left touchline. As Thomond Park adopted its customary silence for kicks, O'Gara later admitted that he had found himself thinking of the match-winning penalty that David Humphreys had missed for Ireland against France the previous season. Sporting a bloodied bandage, Ronan had to wait as Saracens charged out prematurely in a bid to unnerve him, but if it's bottle you're looking for, this guy operates with a full wine rack, and the ball was sent straight over the bar. 'My heart sank when Wood got in for the try because I knew that lad O'Gara was going to convert,' said Mapletoft afterwards. But it wasn't over yet. Saracens roared back in a last-ditch attempt to grab victory, but John Langford somehow found the energy to charge down Lacroix's drop-goal attempt and Munster's progress to the quarter-final stage was guaranteed. 'That was all about character,' said Mick Galwey. 'At 30-24 we should have been dead and buried, but this team never knows when to give up.'

'It was like the old days,' said Moss Keane proudly – a man who had participated in that other famous victory at Thomond Park in 1978. Munster did not need to beat Pontypridd now, but Kidney stressed that victory in Wales was essential to keep the momentum going. Unfortunately, it was not to be, as Munster recorded their first defeat of the campaign. Ironically, Pontypridd did a Munster on Munster, scoring a late try and conversion to steal a 38-36 victory. Although the visitors could argue that they were at the end of a few questionable refereeing decisions, the main objective of qualification had been secured, plus the loss provided Kidney with plenty of ammunition to ward off any cockiness or complacency in his squad.

Mike Mullins *is hauled down by Saracens' Kevin Sorrell. The Munster centre's form that season was outstanding.*

Munster were handed a tough quarter-final draw against the cosmopolitan Parisian team Stade Français, but, crucially, the game would be played at Thomond Park. Less encouraging was the twelve-week break to allow for the Six Nations to be held. However, the majority of the players were involved with either the Senior or A sides during this period, so although not getting match practice with Munster, they were at least playing high-standard rugby. Thankfully, they were also playing winning rugby as both the Senior team and the A team enjoyed successful seasons – the latter outfit coached by Munster's successful tag team of Kidney and O'Donovan.

Nonetheless, there would inevitably be an element of ring-rustiness when they regathered, which, against opponents of the calibre of Stade, could prove fatal. It was for this reason that a friendly against Leicester was organised and, in the circumstances, Munster acquitted themselves very well at Welford Road against a near full-strength Tigers outfit. Kidney rightly stressed that the result itself was of no consequence, and he used some twenty-five players as Munster went down 25-17. It was a cobweb-brushing exercise, and as an opportunity for players to re-familiarise themselves with each other's play, it was extremely worthwhile.

Breath of fresh air: *Killian Keane was unable to break the first-choice centre partnership of Mike Mullins and Jason Holland during Munster's march to Twickenham. However, whenever called upon, as he was against Stade Français at Thomond Park, he always responded superbly.*

There was incredible hype in the build-up to the quarter-final, and the huge number of fans ensured chaos when tickets went on sale. Jason Holland was ruled out of the clash when he and his girlfriend had to travel back to New Zealand following the tragic death of her father. Killian Keane was once again called up, and Munster were fortunate to be able to call on a player of his quality in such sad circumstances. The biggest shock was the omission of Shannon's Alan Quinlan in favour of his club-mate, Eddie Halvey. No one doubted Halvey's God-given abilities, but the fact remained that he was an amateur facing one of the most hard-nosed, professional outfits in the business. He had been offered a professional contract but preferred to continue working rather than devote himself to the oval ball twenty-four hours a day – a decision in keeping with his reputation as something of an enigma. Quinlan had suffered a worrying loss of form and had admitted so himself, saying he had been on a 'downer' since being dropped

ANTHONY FOLEY

BORN: 30/10/1973

Foley is the work-horse of the Munster team: taking on the tough balls, grinding out vital metres to keep his side moving forward, making close-in tackles next to the breakdown. And then there's the unseen work – the lifting in the line-out and closing down space when the opposition spreads the ball from the scrum. These are tasks Anthony Foley willingly undertakes, the chores that make the number eight such a vital cog in the Munster machine.

A legend at St Munchin's where he went to school, Foley was on the Ireland schools side for two years and toured New Zealand in 1992 when Declan Kidney was coach. Foley was always going to emulate his father, Brendan, and join Shannon, and he quickly established himself as part of the invincible Shannon side of the mid-1990s. Impressive performances for club and province saw Foley called up for the first Five Nations match of the 1995 season, at home to England. He was selected as number six, and even though Ireland were comfortably beaten, Foley refused to be overawed and marked the occasion with a try.

He held his place for the rest of the campaign and was part of the World Cup squad later that year. Foley only got one run in that competition, as a sub against Japan, and then was not seen at international level for over a year. Successive defeats at the hands of Australia and Italy saw Foley cast once again into the international wilderness, where he languished for three years. During this period, Shannon and Munster fans could not fathom how Foley's continued excellence at the back of the scrum could be so ignored by the national selectors. The fact that his club-mate, Mick Galwey, was also out in the cold heightened their indignation. However, like Gaillimh, Foley's crucial role in Munster's European Cup assault in 1999/2000 saw him recalled to the Irish side for the game against England

at Twickenham. He was one of the few players to emerge with credit that day and was re-established as Ireland's first-choice number eight.

Although best known for his graft and gruntwork, Foley is a fine footballer and a player who knows the way to the tryline, as he demonstrated repeatedly against Biarritz in 2001. A good judge of the game, he inevitably turns up in the right place at the right time and his performances are characterised by their absence of error. Over the years, the Shannonman has accumulated more man of the match awards than Roy of the Rovers. The only thing that stood against him when it came to selection for the Lions was his height. Being smaller than most of the other players in his position, Foley was not seen as a viable line-out option, even though the Lions first-choice number eight, Scott Quinnell, was never used as a jumper.

As he has been around so long, Foley is often lumped in the Munster veterans' enclosure with Galwey and Clohessy, but Munster and Ireland should hopefully benefit from his consistent brilliance for years to come.

from the Ireland A side. But it was still comforting to know that Munster would have a highly motivated Quinlan on the bench should they need him. While the players were gearing themselves up, Kidney immersed himself in the task of building up Stade. He described them as the 'Manchester United of club rugby', comparing the two clubs on the basis of their collection of foreign stars and domestic dominance. The Munster coach then played down his own team's chances, citing the lengthy break since their last competitive fixture: 'We're in with a shout, that's all', he concluded sombrely.

The Munster shout echoed around Europe as Stade were brushed aside on a wonderful afternoon at Thomond Park. The 27-10 final scoreline was a true reflection of Munster's superiority, with Stade seemingly stunned by the ferocity of the home support and the home side's skill and competitiveness. Dominic Crotty had a superb game: he was assured in defence, dangerous in attack and scored the best try of the game. Anthony Horgan was also on fire, scoring a try and pulling off a tremendous tackle on Stade's Samoan winger Brian Lima at a time when a try would have given the visitors new impetus. The Halvey experiment was an unqualified success. He did tire in the second-half and was replaced by Quinlan, but by that point his athletic jumping at the front of the line had helped wreak havoc on the French line-out, and he had carried out his back-row duties with considerable aplomb.

It was a memorable occasion. The opera singer Suzanne Murphy had given 'There is an Isle' the classical treatment before kick-off, and during the game the Thomond 'choir' gave a stirring rendition of the 'The Fields of Athenry',

which Ronan O'Gara later said had given him 'goosebumps all over'. Afterwards, a tired Eddie Halvey was seen pulling on a cigarette in the dressing-room, and he smiled contentedly before declaring that 'today was a blow for amateur rugby'. Sports hacks sought out Kidney to get his first reaction, and someone reminded the coach of the comparison he had drawn between Stade and Man. United. 'But I never said Manchester United couldn't be beaten', was his matter-of-fact retort.

So we were in the semi-finals, but we still felt like grubby gatecrashers at a particularly swanky party. There were just four teams left in the competition: Toulouse, the hot favourites; Northampton from England; Welsh side Llanelli; and Munster. The draw for the semi-finals was held the day after the Stade match, and it drew horrified gasps from Munster supporters as we were drawn *away* to Toulouse. It was the worst possible scenario. The only people happy

Dominic Crotty had a great day against Stade at Thomond Park, going over here for Munster's second try.

with the pairing were the bookmakers, who stood to lose a fortune if Munster actually won the competition. The match was to be played in Bordeaux, some small consolation for Munster as it meant Toulouse would at least be robbed of the familiarity of their home stadium. But the south of France is the south of France, and some members of the squad had horrific memories of the mauling they had received four years earlier when Toulouse won 60-19. On that occasion there had been a handful of supporters cheering for Munster, this time they would travel in their thousands. But, in truth, deep down

There was a huge scramble for tickets before the quarter-final match with Stade Français. These fans proudly display their tickets after queuing from 5am at the Limerick Sports Store.

There was a wonderful atmosphere at Thomond Park for the game with Stade and the scene was set by opera singer Suzanne Murphy's classical rendition of 'There is an Isle'.

Jason Holland was recalled to the Munster side – no reflection on Killian Keane who had done well against Stade – and Eddie Halvey held on to his place in the back-row in a full-strength Munster line-up.

The bookies saw only one result. Toulouse were a best priced 2-5 while Munster could be taken at 9-4. Nonetheless, the fans made their way to the local Credit Union, and booked their passage to the south of France – if Munster were going to fail, it wouldn't be for the want of shouting.

Toulouse made all the right noises in the build-up: 'We really respect Munster', 'We expect a tough test on Saturday', 'You can never underestimate the Irish, they always play with great fire and passion' ... blah, blah, blah. No surer sign that the home team was not even contemplating defeat.

Gaillimh does his Ginger McLoughlin *impression and drags the Stade Français pack upfield at Thomond Park.*

the fans would admit that they were travelling more in hope than expectation, and the general opinion was that Munster's wonderful adventure was about to come to an end.

On paper, Toulouse looked unbeatable, a team littered with stars, a team with skill and experience. Up front, Califano, Tournaire and Pelous, names bandied about in late-night drunken World XV debates. In the backs, Penaud, Marfaing and Ougier, with the mesmerising Emile N'Tamack on the wing and, just for good measure, the All-Black Lee Stensness, a man who had been instrumental in New Zealand's series win over the Lions in 1993.

This was the first game in the competition when Munster really attracted the attention of the British media, and they were out in force in Bordeaux – after all, there are worse junkets to be sent on. On the Friday before the game, Kidney's men arrived at Stade Lescure for a light run-out. Casually clad in tracksuits and mismatched tops, they laughed and joked their way through a glorified game of tip rugby. Watching English journalists were dumbfounded. 'My God, are they serious about this match?' one was heard to ask. When Toulouse arrived they were fully kitted out and ripped through their drills, all crisp handling and steely-eyed determination. 'Very professional,' said the English hack approvingly. 'I'm afraid your guys are in for a hiding tomorrow.'

Saturday, 6 May 2000. Forty-five minutes to kick-off. Munster take the field for their warm-up and 3,000 Toulouse fans greet their appearance with howls of derision. After posing for a team photograph, Mick Galwey led his men to the end of the ground where the French supporters were gathered most densely. 'I suppose you could say we looked at them and decided to take on the challenge,' said Galwey afterwards, 'just as you do with the All-Blacks and their *haka*.' Munster went through their fifteen-minute warm-up drills while a torrent of abuse rained down on top of them. At the end of the session, Galwey turned and beamed at the Toulouse fans. 'They had given it their best shot and I suppose we had driven them wild. We knew we didn't have to worry about intimidation after that.' It was a defining moment and it set the tone for the afternoon.

Killian Keane, who came in for the unavailable Jason Holland, slips past David Auradou and Cliff Mytton of Stade.

Alan Quinlan may have been dropped for Eddie Halvey against Stade, but he was a great talent to be able to call off the bench and wins a good line-out ball here after entering the fray.

Ronan O'Gara runs at the Toulouse defence on a swelteringly hot day in Bordeaux.

It was a sweltering day, a day for frying eggs on car bonnets, and we feared this would weigh heavily in Toulouse's favour. From the kick-off, the home side threw everything they had at Munster in a bid to blow them away early. The visitors found themselves totally engaged in defence, and it was no surprise when Marfaing knocked over a penalty. But then, after ten minutes, there was a reprieve. A Toulouse handling error allowed Wood to take off on one of his trademark surges. The ball was driven on before being swept out to the right where Crotty and O'Gara sent John Hayes, of all people, crashing over. The score lifted Munster and they threw themselves into their tackling with renewed vigour. Toulouse continued to attack

fiercely, and after a succession of kicks the French went in 15-11 ahead at half-time.

In spite of the scoreline, Toulouse had not played well in the first-half, they looked pedestrian and had committed too many handling errors. But their fans were confident they would improve as the dogged Irish began to wilt under the merciless sun. After all, only fifteen minutes had elapsed when Clohessy was seen squatting on his haunches, gasping for air, and throughout the game Munster had delayed proceedings whenever they could to get their breath and

FRANKIE SHEAHAN
BORN: 27/8/1976

When Frankie Sheahan reflects on the five hookers who took part in the 2001 Lions tour to Australia, he must feel more than a little rueful. While he could not quibble with the selection of the world-class Keith Wood or the versatile Phil Greening, Sheahan is unarguably a better player than the limited Welshman Robyn McBride. And then to watch while Gordon Bulloch of Wales and England's Dorian West were called out to join the tour must have caused considerable pain. But why should Sheahan have felt hard done by when he had only a handful of caps for Ireland and only one as a starter? Quite simply, because the powerfully built Corkman would have had many more caps and much greater exposure had he not had the misfortune to be around when the peerless Keith Wood was in his prime.

Another player who came under the influence of Declan Kidney at PBC, Sheahan played for Munster and Ireland schools teams before joining UCC where he represented the Irish Universities. Already recognised as an exciting young talent, Frankie had the honour of captaining the Irish u21s and was part of the side that won the Triple Crown in 1998. By this stage he had joined Cork Constitution, winning the All-Ireland League title with the Cork club in 1999.

At provincial level, Sheahan first found himself behind former Irish captain Terry Kingston, and when the Dolphin man retired he was up against Mark McDermott of Shannon for the number two jersey. Sheahan was all set for a season as Munster's first-choice hooker when ... cue fanfare ... Keith Wood arrived back from Harlequins. Although it must have been extremely frustrating to be constantly warming the bench, Sheahan never complained and instead took the opportunity to learn from the world's greatest hooker. When he was called upon, as he memorably was during the second-half in Bordeaux against Toulouse, Sheahan showed that his time on the bench had not dulled his appetite for battle. The Irish selectors recognised his quality by selecting him to cover for Wood at international level also.

Unfortunately, what should have been a great experience at Twickenham was marred first by the humiliating defeat to England, and then by an altercation between Sheahan and an Irish supporter at a London hotel after the match. The incident, whilst unsavoury, left Sheahan wiser for the experience, and he was kept on as Ireland's number two number two. When Wood went back to London to fulfil his contract with Harlequins, Sheahan was installed as Munster's first choice. Such was the quality of his play that Wood's absence, seen as a weakness by many pundits, was hardly noticed.

In that season, before the Lions tour, Sheahan was the third-best hooker in Britain and Ireland, behind Wood and Greening. His many fans hoped the Lions selectors would recognise this and grant him a wildcard selection – much as they had done for Barry Williams in 1997. Unfortunately, it was not to be, and once again the outbreak of foot and mouth disease played a part in denying Munster candidates vital high-profile matches. However, Sheahan is young enough to be around for the Lions tour in 2005 and talented enough to take up, once again, where Wood has left off.

O'Gara touches down between the Toulouse posts for Munster's best try of the season after a move that had swept the length of the pitch.

disrupt the French rhythm – a tactic that did not prove popular with the home fans. But there were signs that gave the visitors hope. There was a long walk from the pitch to the dressing-rooms, and in the tunnel Toulouse players were seen sprawled on the ground, some with their boots off. 'They just looked out on their feet,' recalled Clohessy afterwards. 'They threw an awful lot at us in the first-half and I think they shot their bolt.'

Wood did not reappear for the second-half as he had damaged his calf, and Frankie Sheahan burst onto the pitch like an eager young bull into the ring, his appetite whetted by a season of bench-warming. An O'Gara penalty reduced the deficit to 15-14, but then Mike Mullins was sin-binned for disrupting a Toulouse move that looked likely to end in

a score. Wallace was forced to go into the centre in his place. This was the game's critical period when, by rights, the French should have used their numerical advantage to pull away. It never happened. A penalty for each side had the score at 18-17, then, in the 61st minute, Stensness criminally knocked on with a huge overlap outside him. Munster surged back and from a line-out Mullins, Holland and Foley took the ball up. It was switched out to Horgan, who managed to link with the omnipresent Mullins, on to Crotty and O'Gara was over and under the posts. Incredible, or *incroyable* as the dazed Frenchmen might have put it.

Toulouse were stunned, their fans shell-shocked into silence. They had made the two-hour journey from Toulouse in their thousands in expectation of some free-flowing French flair and a comfortable victory. *Mon Dieu!* Everywhere demonic Munster fans were doing their collective nuts, singing, dancing, hugging and kissing. It was Woodstock in red, and it wasn't finished yet, man. Barely two minutes after the O'Gara try, Cazalbou threw out a truly woeful pass that was gleefully intercepted by Holland, and the try and conversion were a mere formality. The score now stood at 31-18 and widespread panic spread through the Toulouse ranks. Desperately they attacked in wave after wave, with Christian Labit particularly menacing, but Wallace and company continued to cut them down, clamber back to their feet and fell them again. Even the sun deserted Toulouse, slinking away for the final ten minutes, and though they managed eventually to force a try through Cazalbou, it was far too late.

Toulouse or not to lose: Jason 'Dutchy' Holland, followed by a beaming O'Gara, ends French hopes after intercepting a loose pass.

Munster's victorious captain Mick Galwey celebrates with the delirious travelling supporters in Bordeaux.

Munster squad member and ex-international Ken O'Connell chairs Peter Stringer off the field at Stade Lescure in Bordeaux.

The following day, revered rugby scribe Stephen Jones described the game in the *Sunday Times*:

> *No matter the capacity in which you are involved in rugby, no matter how jaded your palate, sometimes you see something that reminds you why you fell in love with the game in the first place. On this occasion, the experience was to share in one of Irish rugby's greatest achievements, and one of the biggest upsets in the history of European rugby. The regal stride of the aristocrats of the European club game was cut off at the ankles, and the supporters of Munster, where rugby is a game of the people, celebrated riotously.*

The result stunned everyone, not least Toulouse. 'We expected a tough game, but not that tough,' said N'Tamack. 'I think we made the mistake of assuming that playing the

Très bien, Michel: *Gaillimh receives a warm welcome home at Shannon Airport following the win over Toulouse.*

game in France would be enough.' Assistant coach Daniel Sattamans was even more frank. 'The fear factor wasn't there,' he said. 'Against Montferrand in the quarter-final we felt we were playing against a team that could beat us. That wasn't there against Munster.'

In Ireland, many felt that the victory ranked as high, if not higher than the win over the All-Blacks. 'Character is the hallmark of this side,' said Brian O'Brien. 'I cannot say enough good things about them. They are a wonderful group and a credit to their province and their country.' Now, surely, they would go the whole way. It was pre-ordained. Northampton couldn't get in the way of destiny. They simply couldn't. Could they?

An emotional Mick Galwey carries daughter Neasa in his arms as he walks around Twickenham to pay tribute to the Munster fans following the loss to Northampton.

CHAPTER FOUR

FINAL AGONY

W e are not comfortable with the tag of favourites in Ireland. Traditionally, we are far more at ease in the role of underdog, which gives us the possibility of glorious failure (1916 Rising) or shock victory (Dana, Eurovision 1970). Therefore, when Irish bookmakers listed Munster as favourites for the European Cup final against Northampton at Twickenham, it led to a distinct feeling of unease among Munster fans.

After the mauling of Toulouse, bandwagon syndrome was in full swing. All those who had decided not to travel to Bordeaux because of the expense and the expectation of defeat were determined to atone by going to Twickenham. The vast amount of publicity post-Toulouse had seeped through to the uninitiated, with the result that even those who thought 'rolling mauls' were something to do with plasticine manipulation were confidently predicting victory over the English. All very worrying. The consensus seemed to be that after a succession of last-gasp victories, allied to the manner in which the 'impossible' had been achieved in Bordeaux, Declan Kidney's team had God Almighty himself on their side and they were going to take the trophy.

Kidney tried to keep the collective feet of his side rooted to *terra firma*, but it was impossible not to be swept along by the hype. Of course, this played into Northampton's hands. They had scraped into the final past Llanelli, courtesy of an injury-time penalty from the metronomic Paul Grayson. They also had to contend with a ridiculously congested fixture list in the build-up to the final, whereas Munster had the luxury of a three-week lay-off. Not only were the Saints contesting the Tetley's Bitter Cup final against Wasps, they were also bidding to qualify for the following season's European Cup campaign, which necessitated playing a number of Premiership games in quick succession. Their manager, John Steele, cited all these disadvantages as reasons why Munster were favourites, but we were not fooled. This was a seriously good Northampton side, which boasted skill and experience in equal abundance.

In the front-row was the gargantuan Scot Mattie Stewart, the mighty Argentinian hooker Federico Mendez and the raw power of South African prop Gary Pagel. The second-row boasted Tim Rodber, who had caps for England and the Lions and a jaw that might have been chiselled out

of Mount Rushmore. Then, in the back-row, there was Scottish international Budge Pountney and the peerless Samoan Pat Lam at number eight. The options in the backs made for equally grim reading. Not only could the Saints parade the sublime skills of Allan Bateman in the centre,

The Munster squad *that contested the European Cup final at Twickenham in 2000.*

they could also call on England scrum-half and captain Matt Dawson and his international colleague, the powerful wing Ben Cohen. And if that wasn't enough to instil doubt, nay fear, they had one of the deadliest exponents of dead-ball kicking in the world: Paul Grayson.

Nonetheless, ever-optimistic Munster fans proceeded with their plans for the mass pilgrimage to London. A group of us decided to travel *Auf Wiedersehen Pet* style in a battered old van. The plan was to get the ferry from Rosslare to Bristol, dump the van there (not literally) and travel to London by train on the morning of the game. Sounded great in theory. All over the province similar schemes were drawn up, although the majority of fans seemed to prefer to fly and numerous chartered flights were arranged. As match day approached the frenzy intensified. Tickets were snapped up as soon as they became available, and it was evident that the province would be emptied for this seismic clash.

In the Irish and British media, all possible angles on the game were analysed and then re-analysed. Everybody from Jeremy Guscott to Jimmy the Shoe-shiner was canvassed for their opinions on the likely result and, worryingly, most plumped for Munster. The closer we got to 27 May the more the fates seemed to conspire against Northampton. First they lost to Wasps in the Cup final, a result that could be taken two ways: it would either increase self-doubt in the Northampton camp or strengthen their resolve to avoid another Twickenham defeat. Then, a week-and-a-half before match day, the Saints were dealt a double body-blow when Matt Dawson and Nick Beal were both injured in a league defeat to Saracens. Dawson damaged his shoulder while Beal was definitely ruled out after he broke his tibia and fibia in his right shin. Dawson was sent for scans on his shoulder, but, effectively, Northampton began to plan the final minus their most influential player.

Kidney now had a nightmare task to try and stem the rising tide of optimism, and he strove manfully to do so. 'I'd like to talk to the people who are saying we are favourites,' said the Munster coach. 'The Northampton pack are collectively sixteen stone heavier than Toulouse. They are, in fact, the biggest side we will play all season.' The coach's valiant effort to ease the pressure on his side was not matched by the actions of all his players. Anthony Foley

was quoted in the papers confidently proclaiming that it was, 'time for my father and the Munster team who beat the All-Blacks in 1978 to move over'. It is hard to tell whether this was said tongue-in-cheek or not, but one can only speculate as to the reaction of the notoriously cagey Kidney to his number eight's verbosity when he collared him behind closed doors. Meanwhile, the Northampton players were falling over themselves in their eagerness to talk up Munster. 'We will go into the match very much the underdog,' said Tim Rodber, 'but we are happy to be in that position. Losing someone as influential as Matt Dawson is obviously a big blow.'

Munster announced an unchanged side from the one that defeated Toulouse. There had been doubts about the fitness of Keith Wood, but the mighty hooker was down to start the final. Northampton's team, despite their injury problems, appeared ominously strong. The team was: P Grayson, C Moir, A Bateman, M Allen, B Cohen, A Hepher, D Malone, G Pagel, F Mendez, M Stewart, A Newman, T Rodber, D Mackinnon, B Pountney, P Lam. The injury to Beal meant Grayson was given a starting role at full-back. Frankly, we would have preferred to see Beal playing, as this looked like a match that would be decided by place-kicking and Grayson was one of the best in the business. Also, there was the issue of John Hayes versus Pagel in the front-row. Hayes was having a wonderful season, but there were still questionmarks over his scrummaging technique – questions that Pagel would be asking forcibly.

Putting these worrying thoughts to one side, on Friday lunchtime the *Auf Wiedersehen Pet* crew threw their sleeping bags into the back of our (t)rusty van and headed for Rosslare. There was a wonderful sense of adventure on the ferry to Fishguard. Red jerseys were everywhere, and not just the modern Munster variety. Many players and ex-players had fished out their tattered old Munster schools jerseys for the occasion, and the Cork GAA strip was also much in evidence. Predictably, the entire Munster contingent congregated by the bar, and despite our group's best efforts to maintain a cautious note, the overwhelming consensus was that victory was guaranteed on the morrow. Several pints later we were agreeing wholeheartedly on everything and leading rousing choruses of 'You'll never beat the Irish' ... so much for caution.

The drive to Bristol from Fishguard in the early hours of Saturday morning was long but painless, courtesy of the aforementioned pints. A word of warning, however: should you ever decide to employ the *Auf Wiedersehen Pet* mode of travel, be prepared, five men confined in one van do not create the most wholesome of odours. After grabbing a few hours' sleep in Bristol, we finally abandoned the trusty, musty, rusty van and boarded the train.

London. Although only six hours away from kick-off, there was none of the atmosphere you would normally associate with big match days. The English broadsheets we purchased for the train journey only covered the final on the inside sports pages, preferring to lead off with England's soccer friendly against Brazil. Nor were there any other Munstermen on the train, although we did spot one portly, middle-aged chap in a Northampton jersey and proceeded to growl at him menacingly. Red jerseys were conspicuously absent upon arrival in London also. We had conceitedly thought that the Munster invasion would overwhelm England's capital, but had failed to factor in the sheer enormity of the place. Our red jerseys merited no more than an occasional bored glance as Londoners continued about their daily business. All very deflating for those of us trying to get psyched up for the occasion.

Boarding the tube for Richmond, we still failed to spy any fellow Monsters. What was going on? Did we have the right day? Should we be in Cardiff? or Paris? And then we found them. Richmond was awash with red. Munster fans were everywhere, laughing, shouting and greeting familiar faces. A huge surge of adrenaline swept over us. This was more like it. Two-and-a-half hours to kick-off ... pub. We entered a typical English hostelry. On the corner it was titled The Crown & Anchor or something similar, it had slot machines, Sky Sports and pork scratchings: what more could you want? There was a wonderful atmosphere at this stage – we may have been in Richmond, but it could just as easily have been Cork or Limerick. Forty minutes later, suitably fortified, the fans headed *en masse* for the stadium.

Twickenham is a wonderful example of all you could ask of a modern stadium: easy to negotiate, with wide spaces for freedom of movement, it also has numerous toilets, bars and food vendors. The pitch area is vast, but the high,

Eddie Halvey *tries to break through the Saints' defence at Twickenham.*

Gaillimh is held *by Allan Bateman and Ben Cohen. His sin-binning was a boost to Northampton at a crucial stage of the game.*

encircling stands create a cauldron effect you just cannot achieve at windswept Lansdowne Road. We still had an hour-and-a-half to kick-off, but the fans were streaming in. We joined a throng of Monsters at a bar under the stands, and things really began to hot up.

At this stage, there were plenty of Saints fans in the same area and the banter was lively but civilised. Then suddenly, from one of the bars further down the line, came the first few notes of 'The Fields of Athenry'. The song swept along the Munster fans like a bush fire and soon it was being roared out. The Northampton followers valiantly attempted to respond with 'When the Saints go Marching in', but, God bless them, 'twas like Sonny Knowles trying to follow Bruce Springsteen. First blood to the Reds, and it was out to our seats, high in the southern stand.

The Twickenham pitch looked truly marvellous, it was a fitting stage for a match of this magnitude. The only

criticism of the occasion was the organisers' mistaken belief that they had a duty to whip the crowd up into a frenzy. As a result we had to endure a truly awful PA announcer bombarding us with moronic cheerleading and ear-splitting pop music. He was reminiscent of those awful 'Is everybody having a good tiiiimmmme?' travel reps you encounter on cheap sun holidays – all forced gaiety and no substance and, on this occasion, totally superfluous. A crowd of that size and with that amount of anticipation (and alcohol) will obviously generate its own atmosphere. Even the arrival of our red heroes onto the pitch was marred by the PA saboteur: 'LET'S HEAR IT FOR THE MEN FROM MUUUUNNNNSSSSTTTEERRRR!' Groan. The Gladiatorial entry ruined by a prattling idiot.

Putting the PA hell to one side we settled down ... the waiting was finally over. This was it. As Foley would put it, it was time for the Munster team of 1978 to move over.

KEITH WOOD
BORN: 27/7/1972

Where do you start with this guy? Keith Wood is without doubt the best hooker of his generation and one of the best of all time – only Sean Fitzpatrick of New Zealand could really compete with him for that title. When he won his first cap in Australia in 1994, Bob Dwyer said he had the potential to be the best in the world, and he was proved right. On the Lions tour to South Africa in 1997, Woody was one of the main reasons the series was won – he was a constant thorn in the side of the Boks. Then, four years later in Australia, he was the outstanding Lion on tour: powerful in the scrummage, punishing in the tackle and an omnipresent force in the loose. Woody's performance in the first Test will go down in history as one of the greatest individual displays ever given by a Lion. The fact that his father, Gordon, had represented the Lions with distinction meant a great deal to Keith, and his determination to carry on his family's proud tradition was reflected on and off the pitch.

Hailing from County Clare, his first love as a youngster was hurling. He began playing rugby during his time at St Munchin's College, but achieved no representative honours. However, even then his mobility was such that he frequently played in the back-row. On leaving school he joined Garryowen and it was then Wood really began to get noticed. This was still the era when front-rows largely moved from one set-piece to the next, but not Woody. It would not be exaggerating to say he patented the idea of hookers taking on pop balls close to rucks, certainly in Irish rugby it was a strange phenomenon. Wood had the speed and the footballing agility to equal any back, and he began to earn rave notices in the early 1990s, culminating in selection to the Munster u20 side.

When the game went professional, Wood, like many of his international colleagues, crossed the Irish Sea and joined Harlequins in London. There his profile increased tenfold.

Intelligent and charismatic, Woody became one of the most recognised figures in world rugby and one of the game's biggest earners.

Wood first captained Ireland against Australia in 1996 and, always forthright in his views, in his post-match interview stated bluntly that losing respectably to Southern Hemisphere teams was no longer good enough, and that he expected more from his side. However, the majority of his international career has been spent in defeat, and it was only in 2000 that he began to get used to the feeling of victory in the green shirt.

Due to the length of time he had to spend with the Irish squad for the 1999 World Cup, Wood was able to secure a one-year release from his Harlequins contract and he came home and joined Munster. Whatever his feelings towards the province earlier in his career, Woody now threw himself wholeheartedly into Munster's assault on Europe. Certain memories will always stand out: his winning try in the nail-biting win over Saracens at Thomond; the breathtaking run in Bordeaux that forced him to retire, injured, for the second-half; and his relentless surging at the Northampton defence at Twickenham, which was, unfortunately, all in vain. Even if he never dons the red jersey again, Wood will always be regarded as one of Munster's own. His continued success on the world stage is greeted with pride in his home province.

There's no way *Munster full-back Dominic Crotty is letting go of Northampton out-half Ali Hepher.*

David Wallace *celebrates his try, the only one of the game, with team-mate Anthony Horgan.*

What unfolded over the next two hours was a very strange game for Munster followers to fathom. Firstly, Ronan O'Gara was struggling, as was his half-back partner Peter Stringer. We had become so used to Ronan's all-round excellence that it was entirely unexpected to see him so out of sorts. He had accumulated 131 points in the competition to date and would finish as the top scorer, yet he drew a blank that afternoon, missing four kicks and a couple of drop-goal attempts. The Northampton back-row of Lam, Pountney and Mackinnon was putting the Munster half-backs under enormous pressure, which stifled the entire backline. Similarly, in the scrums Pagel was turning the screw on Hayes and giving Lam the perfect platform from which to operate. We were under the cosh, but, despite a couple of shaky moments, our defence seemed to be holding.

Then Woody made one of his trademark surges, the ball was flashed left and the ubiquitous David Wallace powered over in the corner. The Monsters went wild. We may have only two chants, 'The Fields of Athenry' and 'Munster, clap, clap, clap, Munster', but by God, they were belted out now with renewed gusto. 'Dutchy' Holland then dropped a goal and suddenly we were 8-6 in front and so it stayed until half-time. The try and the continued excellence of the defence gave us confidence, but on the negative side the forwards were under the most pressure they had endured all season.

The second-half continued in much the same vein: Northampton pounding away, Munster plugging the dyke. O'Gara had a kick blocked down and though the ball was recovered, Munster were penalised for not releasing. Grayson kicked the penalty, and now we were behind by a point. Not to worry, we reassured ourselves, the boys will fight back, they always do. Then Dom Malone, the scrum-half who was playing so well that Dawson was hardly missed, intercepted an O'Gara pass and set off on a sixty-yard dash for the line. Eddie Halvey set off in pursuit, and though Malone is no slouch, the Shannonman's supreme athleticism was demonstrated by a superb chase and tackle. Surely that was a sign, we reasoned ... and then Gaillimh was sin-binned for obstruction.

This was catastrophic. Not only were we down a man for ten whole minutes but we had also lost our captain, talisman and most experienced player. Predictably, Northampton increased the pressure. On average, a sin-binning is calculated to be worth nine points to the opposition, and the Saints set out to prove the statisticians correct. Courageously, the thinned red line continued to hold out. The Munster fans counted down the ten minutes, watching Gaillimh pacing the touchline impatiently. Finally, after an eternity, he was waved back on.

The reappearance of the legend from Currow was the signal for the biggest cheer of the day. There was still time. C'MMONNNN MUNNSSTEERRRR! One minute of normal time left and we were awarded a penalty out on the left-hand touchline. Dèjà vu. It was Saracens all over again. This was O'Gara's forte, he'd been here before, with a proven big-match temperament. What a way to win the European Cup: Galwey returns after being unjustly sin-binned and O'Gara kicks the winning penalty in the last minute to beat the English on their own patch.

Northampton Saints 9 Munster 8

Heineken Cup

The scoreboard *tells a sad story as Munster battles for line-out possession with the clock ticking down.*

Ronan lines up the ball, same as always. He looks up at the post, runs in and strikes it sweetly, same as always. The ball sails majestically towards the centre of the posts. From our position behind the goal-line it looks perfect. In fact, it's beautiful, it's stunning, it's poetry ... it's wide.

And that, effectively, was that. Three or four minutes later the final whistle sounded and thousands of Munster supporters looked at each other in confusion. It wasn't supposed to end like this. This wasn't the script. Where was the winning try from Woody in the dying seconds? What the hell was going on?

Everywhere Northampton players and supporters were going mad, goaded on by that tosser on the PA system. We couldn't begrudge the Saints their success. They had produced a very professional display, turning the screw up front and expertly curbing any Munster attempt at creativity out wide. On top of that, although they had many big-name stars, it was an old-fashioned club with old-fashioned values. They played their home games at a traditional rugby ground and not at some half-empty soccer stadium with tennis tramlines for goal-line areas. Maybe if it had been Wasps or Saracens we would have been bitter, but as it was we were just bitterly disappointed.

MICK GALWEY
BORN: 8/10/1966

Galwey's role in Munster's wonderful adventure cannot be overstated. Captain of the team, he is the type of man others instinctively follow, and the big man from Currow in County Kerry is revered in Munster, and indeed Irish, rugby circles.

It is very hard to believe that at the time of the 1999 World Cup, Galwey was the forgotten man of Irish rugby. His last start in an Irish shirt had come in the embarassing defeat to Western Samoa in 1996. For much of the 1990s, international selectors tended to be sizeist, and it was felt that Galwey, at 6ft 4ins, was simply not tall enough to meet the requirements of an international lock-forward. He had been tried at back-row for Ireland, but without great success. Yet his many followers down south who had witnessed Gaillimh's consistent excellence for Shannon and Munster could not fathom his absence from the international side, especially during the grim 1990s when defeat was the norm. Friends from Castleisland RFC in Kerry, where Galwey cut his teeth, reckon the big man has been dropped thirteen times by his country – surely a record.

Growing up in Kerry, it was natural that he should play Gaelic, and his footballing ability was such that he won an All-Ireland medal as part of the Kerry squad in 1986. He first played rugby with the junior club Castleisland before joining Shannon, and it wasn't long before he was wearing the red of Munster. He was with the Irish squad that toured France in 1988 and scored a famous victory in Auch over what was, in all but name, the full national side. Galwey's first cap, in 1991, again saw him take on the French, and between then and the start of the 1995 season he was first choice for his country. He was passed over for the 1995 World Cup in South Africa, the selectors preferring to take Davy Tweed of Ballymena.

By the time of the 1999 World Cup, Gaillimh had been discarded once more, in spite of his continued excellence for Munster. Declan Kidney had recognised that Galwey was the man to lead the province forward at a time when a host of youngsters were being blooded. To the delight of his many fans, Gaillimh captained the province to victory over the national side in Musgrave Park in the run-up to the World Cup, turning in a monumental display. Ireland's poor showing in the World Cup and the humiliation at Twickenham at the start of the Six Nations Championship opened the way for an international recall at the ripe old age of thirty-three.

Gaillimh's experience was crucial as the Kerryman and his Munster colleagues helped their country reproduce the magic they had been conjuring at provincial level. He has adapted marvellously to the professional regime and, along with his long-time colleague Peter Clohessy, has proven that age is no barrier to excellence. He received the honour of captaining his country for the first time against Romania in June 2001, at the age of thirty-four.

There is no doubt that Galwey's inspirational leadership has been vital in Munster's success, but this tends to overshadow his playing abilities. Supremely strong , with soft hands and footballing skills betraying his Gaelic background, he is also a very intelligent player and rarely takes the wrong option on the pitch. These qualities earned him selection on the 1993 Lions tour to New Zealand, one of only two Irish players in the original party.

Galwey has remained modest and unassuming despite all the adulation he receives. His remarkable resurrection when many had written him off has guaranteed Gaillimh's status as an Irish sporting legend.

Northampton's *Paul Grayson, who kicked the winning points for the English side, commiserates with Mike Mullins, Mick Galwey and Peter Stringer, while John Langford lies back on the Twickenham grass.*

John Langford *is totally dejected as he struggles to come to terms with Munster's defeat at the final hurdle.*

Out on the pitch a strange scene was unfolding. The Northampton players had embarked on a lap of honour, jumping and jostling each other in celebration. In the centre of the park the entire Munster squad were gathered in a tightly knit circle, arms intertwined. Television pictures showed Peter Bracken, a fringe member of the squad but a huge young talent, with tears cascading down his cheeks. At the centre of the circle was Kidney, moving about, gesticulating, shouting at his players. What was he saying? 'I told them to be proud of what they had achieved,' recalls Kidney. 'We knew it would take a very good side to beat us, and Northampton are a very good side, so there is no disgrace in that. I told them to go over and thank the fans with their heads held high.' And they did. 'The Fields of Athenry' was given one last almighty rendition as they made their way around the pitch. At this stage, Gaillimh was carrying his daughter Neasa on his shoulders, and quite honestly there wasn't a dry eye in the stands. This was no time for cynicism. This team had given us a wonderful year, they had brought us tremendous joy and it was time we let them know how much we appreciated them.

Big, grizzly men stared fixedly ahead, pretending to blow their noses for fear their companions would catch them with moist eyes and slag them afterwards. Out on the pitch, John Hayes stood out, as always. 'The Bull' was walking slightly to one side and staring into the stands with what seemed to be an expression of wonderment. Hayes embodied everything that was good about this team. This was not a side of Flash Harrys, it was about hard work and commitment combined with skill and intelligence. Hayes had been put under enormous pressure in the tight that afternoon, but had still found the energy to turn in his customary mighty performance in the close-quarter exchanges at ruck and maul. These were our heroes, and standing and applauding them was the only way we could let these men know that that was how we regarded them – heroes one and all.

There was a slightly unreal atmosphere outside the ground afterwards. Familiar faces were hailed, but not in the excited way that would have marked a famous victory. Instead there was a funereal air hanging over the red hordes. Groups stood, heads bent, on the thronged roads, analysing the match and where it had all gone wrong. Alcohol brought no release. There was still a sense of adventure in being gathered *en masse* in a foreign country, but none of the fevered excitement that only victory brings.

The train back to Bristol was full of rowdy England soccer supporters celebrating their highly creditable 1-1 draw with Brazil, so we kept a low profile by the bar. We hit Bristol inebriated and still donned proudly in red, and decided to paint the West country city the same colour.

Anthony Foley, *after producing his customary wholehearted performance, ruefully reflects on defeat.*

The fact that this almost happened quite literally with Munster blood can be blamed on the Bristolians failure to appreciate the Irish sense of humour. The Bristol accent has that sing-song quality that immediately conjures up images of country yokels with bits of straw hanging out of their mouths. It's all 'Oiy be a farmer, oiy be', and so forth. Surprisingly, when a drunk Munsterman fell into the Gents in one public house and roared out, 'Oiy loikes Armadillos', the large group of country yokels didn't fall around in uncontrollable mirth. Unlike the drunk Munsterman and his friends.

All in all, an ignominious end to an ignominious day. The mood of melancholy persisted all the way down the motorway to the ferry. Once again the boat was crowded with fans, but the energy and vitality that marked the trip over was replaced by lethargy and listlessness. As the long journey home began, the bar was relatively empty whereas the relaxation lounges were doing a roaring trade as the majority of supporters slept or played cards. But an hour playing cards felt like an eternity, so it was off to the bar to see if it had picked up any. It had.

The room was now crowded with fans drowning their sorrows. Once again the match was mulled over and the sense of regret was overwhelming. Gradually, however, the mood began to alter subtly. The decibel level began to rise, and more and more bodies filtered in, abandoning the cards for the *craic*. The sense of unity that characterised this wonderful band of supporters slowly began to reassert itself. Strangers we may have been, but we were united in our mutual love of Munster.

Then, a lone voice rang out: 'By a lonely prison wall, I heard a young man calling.' The words had been sung countless times that weekend, but now they served as a salve to our wounds, a moment of catharsis to relieve us of the burden of our sorrow. It brought an end to the grieving process. Everyone abandoned their conversations and roared out the 'Fields' as though their lives depended on it. Indeed, the unfortunates who sang 'Nearer my God to Thee' on the sinking *Titanic* (when their lives did depend on it) could not have sung with greater fervour than the Munster crowd on the Sealink that Sunday. So we had lost. So what? We were still the best team in Europe, feck it, in the world. And we'd be back. You could count on that.

Keith Wood and Peter Clohessy salute their fans as they take a lap of Twickenham.

RONAN O'GARA

BORN: 7/3/1977

If one player above any other has become a star on the back of Munster's performances, it is Corkman Ronan O'Gara. When Declan Kidney began selecting him as Munster's first-choice out-half there were few outside knowledgeable rugby circles in Munster who would have heard of him. Just a few years later, O'Gara was recognised as one of Europe's top number tens, and had secured a berth on the 2001 Lions tour to Australia.

O'Gara first encountered Kidney during his time at PBC. He then went to UCC, but spent only one season playing for the college before joining Cork Constitution, the team he had played for as a youngster. While it is his place-kicking that tends to grab the headlines, there is a lot more to his game than the ability to kick goals. His kicking out of hand is also exemplary and his defensive game is underrated. But perhaps his greatest quality is his speed of passing. During Munster's run at the European Cup final in 1999/2000, O'Gara ran the show. His injury-time kick from the left-hand touchline against Saracens at Thomond Park was a remarkable tribute to his coolness under pressure, and his try against Toulouse in Bordeaux will surely go down as one of the highlights of his career. His form for Munster saw him selected against England in the first Six Nations match of 2000.

Perhaps fortunately for him, injury ruled him out and so he missed the mauling at Twickenham, but won his first cap in the next match against Scotland at Lansdowne Road. Although he experienced a few ropey moments in that game, O'Gara nonetheless came through with his reputation enhanced. Since then he has been Ireland's first-choice out-half, amassing points and oozing assurance every time he dons the green jersey.

Credited with doing so much to get them there, it was tragic that O'Gara's worst day in a Munster jersey should have come against Northampton in the European Cup final. It wasn't just the missed penalty that could have won it, O'Gara looked ill at ease throughout, having been targetted by his English opponents. However, he bounced back and his superb form for Munster and Ireland forced the Lions selectors to sit up and take notice.

His selection on that tour was entirely merited, and although one could not argue with the fact that the supremely gifted Jonny Wilkinson was first choice, the experience he gained was of immense benefit to the Corkman. Unfortunately, O'Gara was not treated fairly on the tour and his progression was thwarted at every opportunity. Coach Graham Henry hinted that the selectors had made a mistake in failing to select the Scot Gregor Townsend as one of the out-halves. All of this must have been hard to take for the young Corkman, but, unlike others, he never complained. When given a chance on tour, O'Gara's form was good, particularly in attack, and he learned much, including the need to introduce a greater physical element to his game.

Despite his consistently good play, undoubtedly the most oft-quoted event of his tour will be the brutal attack perpetrated upon him by the cowardly Ducan McRae in the match against New South Wales. The ferocity of the attack was unprecedented, but O'Gara showed remarkable restraint in the aftermath and his dignity in the face of adversity won him many new admirers.

In spite of the adulation and attention that has come his way, O'Gara remains pleasantly self-effacing. This level-headed attitude, together with his excellent all-round abilities, could see him remembered as the greatest Munster and Irish out-half of all time.

MUNSTER XV v. NORTHAMPTO

PETER CLOHESSY 1

KEITH

MICK GALWEY 4

EDDIE HALVEY 6

ANTHONY

PETER STRINGER 9

ANTHONY HORGAN 11

MIKE MULLINS 12

DOMINIC

at TWICKENHAM, 27 MAY 2000

3

WOOD

JOHN HAYES

5

JOHN LANGFORD

7

DAVID WALLACE

FOLEY

10

RONAN O'GARA

13

14

JASON HOLLAND

JOHN KELLY

CROTTY

The Munster fans, or 'Monsters' as they came to be known, are recognised as the best fans in Europe. A crowd of 30,000 made their way to Twickenham for the European Cup final, and this particular group certainly enjoyed the experience.

THE M

CHAPTER FIVE

GHTY MONSTERS

The Munster story is as much about the fans as it is about the players and backroom staff. The way the public has taken to this Munster team has been, quite simply, astounding. Munster had always been well supported for the visits of major touring sides, but never before had so many turned out to witness Interprovincial matches. Now, prior to big European Cup games, even training sessions draw attendances of several hundred.

It has all been something of an overnight sensation. Up until the start of season 1999/2000, attendances for Munster's European Cup ties were decent but unremarkable, while the numbers for Interprovincials were downright poor. In the first Cup tie at home to Pontypridd, it was not hard to get access to Thomond Park as an audience of less than 3,000 watched the match in comfort on the uncrowded terraces. But by the end of that season, 30,000 people travelled to London to support the men in red in the European Cup final, prompting Declan Kidney to comment drily: 'We are told there will be something like 79,000 in Twickenham, the nearest we have come to that is the 79 that were in Dooradoyle for the game against Connacht last season.'

What had happened to bring about this remarkable transformation?

The team's approach to the game and their subsequent success captured the imagination of the sports-loving fans in the province, and many of those who started attending rugby matches that season were doing so for the first time. It was a mutually beneficial arrangement: the fans loved roaring on a team winning against the odds while their lusty support enabled

Munster captain *Gaillimh is revered by Munster supporters, seen here mobbing their hero after the momentous win over Saracens at Thomond Park.*

Munster to do just that. There is no doubt that the crowd has inspired the team to many crucial victories when the day seemed lost. Think of the cliffhanger win over Saracens at Thomond, or the 3,000 devotees who roared their team to victory in Bordeaux, or the thronged masses, again in Thomond, when the Biarritz offensive threatened to overwhelm Munster. It was the tremendous support that inspired them to hold on.

The Munster fans have become famous throughout Europe for their fervour and dedication to their side. After the win over Newport in Wales in 2001, the Newport club president paid homage to the visiting supporters: 'The level of Munster support was amazing, they have the best fans in Europe.' The red horde was truly immense that evening. Rodney Parade was known as something of a fortress in the principality, a notoriously intimidating venue for the opposition. The Newport fans prided themselves on their boisterous support and the atmosphere they generated within the ground, but on that night they admitted to being bowled over by the magnificent display from the Munster faithful.

It is when they begin to sing that the Munster fans are really overwhelming. The song that will always be associated with this team more than any other is, rather bizarrely, 'The Fields of Athenry'. Bizarre given that the fields of the title reside in County Galway, in the rival province of Connacht. But the Monsters have made it their own.

Before big European Cup games *there were bigger crowds at Munster's training sessions than there had been for matches a few years previously. Here, Anthony Foley signs autographs for fans at Thomond Park before the semi-final with Toulouse.*

Fans queue in William Street, Limerick, for tickets to the quarter-final match with Stade Français in 2000. Unfortunately, many genuine supporters lost out as the corporate sector moved in on the Munster success story.

The song was routinely sung by the Connacht team after famous victories in the European Shield when Warren Gatland was their coach, and it is more usually associated with the Celtic football team in Scotland. Much as England can trace their adoption of 'Swing Low Sweet Chariot' to Chris Oti's three tries against Ireland at Twickenham in 1988, so can Munster trace their embezzlement of the 'Fields' to the Stade Français quarter-final at Thomond Park. There was a break in play with Munster awarded a penalty, and the song began in one corner of the ground, gathered momentum and swelled into a magnificent crescendo before Ronan O'Gara knocked over a penalty to the sound of deathly silence.

The other song that has played a major role in this story is the one penned by Brian O'Brien when he was managing the team. Using the tune of 'El Toreador' from Bizet's *Carmen*, O'Brien wrote some rousing lyrics. The result, 'Stand Up and Fight', is now routinely belted out in the Munster dressing-room after victory has been secured.

In the midst of the growing Munster hype, the very talented John Breen wrote the play *Alone it Stands*, a celebration of Munster's win over the All-Blacks in 1978. Comprising a cast of only six actors, this wonderful production boasted a fantastically witty script and truly amazing choreography. The play has since played to packed houses everywhere, including to the entire Munster squad, and has won the praise of theatre critics and ordinary fans alike.

By the time of the Newport game, the large travelling support-base for Declan Kidney's team had

DAVID WALLACE

BORN: 8/7/1976

David Wallace was always going to be a rugby star. There was the family precedent for starters – older brothers Richard and Paul had gone to the very top and represented Ireland and the Lions. The youngest Wallace had the talent and the right attitude to emulate their success. By the time the game went open in the autumn of 1995, David was just nineteen years old and one of the new breed of young rugby players determined to forge a career in the professional game.

A squad member with Garryowen in Limerick, Wallace had played with the Irish u21s and had been selected for Ireland's gruelling development tour to New Zealand in 1997, where he played all seven games and returned with his reputation considerably improved. The Munster back-row was a highly competitive area, with the likes of Alan Quinlan, Eddie Halvey and Colm McMahon to contend with, but by 1999/2000 Wallace was the first-choice number seven.

His performances in the red jersey were consistently excellent and he quickly became one of the first names on the team-sheet. Not a traditional, scavenging openside in the mould of a Back or a Kronfeld, Wallace used his powerful physique and experience as a number eight in club rugby to become one of the best ball-carrying forwards in Europe. He was instrumental in Munster's march to the European Cup final, and scored the only try against Northampton at Twickenham. That summer he won his first cap against Argentina during Ireland's tour to the Americas. The following season his form was just as good and his performance against Castres in a rainy Musgrave Park was quite simply magnificent.

Wallace began the Six Nations as Ireland's first-choice openside, and two superb displays in the wins over Italy and France had him earmarked for the Lions tour to Australia.

Unfortunately, the foot and mouth crisis and his own leg injury crisis intervened. Although he recovered in time for Munster's semi-final in Lille, Wallace was clearly not match-fit and was not selected for the Lions squad. However, injury to Lawrence Dallaglio saw Wallace called into the squad, and he finally and deservedly emulated his older brothers by donning the famous red jersey.

Against ACT Brumbies, Wallace showed the Lions selectors what they had missed out on, but was nevertheless passed over for the Test squad. With Neil Back clearly losing the battle of the scavengers against George Smith, many argued that Wallace should be included for the Third Test. Even former England stalwart Jeff Probyn betrayed his John Bull image and said the Munsterman should be favoured over his own countryman. Sadly, it was not to be, and once again Back was outclassed, with Smith helping the Wallabies to clinch the series. However, Wallace has time on his side, and Munster's finest openside has the talent and the ambition to go on and challenge Fergus Slattery for the title of Ireland's finest number seven.

become the norm. However, the famous day in 2000 in Bordeaux against Toulouse was the first occasion when the supporters really travelled in their thousands. In the week prior to that semi-final the Irish media was full of stories about the fans and the lengths they were willing to go to for their beloved Munster. One Limerick supporter was unable to travel for financial reasons – he was getting married the following week and was cash-strapped. He had attended every single game prior to the semi-final and so he was understandably distraught. In an attempt to convey his grief, and his continuing support, he sent the following fax to the team hotel: 'I'm proud to be associated with the team and I can promise you I will be at the final ... married, single or divorced.'

Then there is the story of two lads from Limerick, Kevin O'Dwyer and Mike 'Gunners' Cunningham, who undertook to make their way to Bordeaux by motorcycle. At 6am on the Thursday before the match they left the Hurlers pub in Limerick, and over the next forty-eight hours they travelled to Rosslare, got the

ferry to Fishguard, on to Dover, got the ferry to Calais, and then biked down the length of France before eventually arriving at Bordeaux. The gruelling nature of the lads' journey made the eventual victory all the sweeter.

There is no doubt the ardour of the fans is hugely appreciated by the team itself, and Kidney is always at pains to point out that he and his men are grateful for the sacrifices, financial and otherwise, made in order to follow Munster.

Modern rugby has become increasingly commercialised and there is a certain amount of corporate hijacking of big games at home. It becomes trendy to attend these games, and people who don't really know what they are talking about can be heard braying loudly about the merits of the team, usually to impress clients or to justify their position on the bandwagon. It was an unfortunate side-effect of Munster's success that the clamour for tickets could sometimes leave the genuine fan out in the cold. There were many accounts of long-serving supporters being unable to get tickets to big games as the corporate sector gobbled up whatever they could. However, it is on the away trips that the true die-hard fans come to the fore. Much in the same way as followers of Jack Charlton's Irish team willingly placed themselves in debt in order to follow their footballing heroes, so too did Munstermen cancel holidays and household purchases simply to be there for their team.

It is a situation that can only be envied by the other provinces. On the way to their European title in 1999, Ulster packed out Ravenhill and Lansdowne Road, but their fans were practically non-existent on the road. Similarly, Leinster could expect a full house at Donnybrook for their Friday night games (as the Dublin 4 set wolfed down their cappuccinos after work and enjoyed a bit of rugger before hitting the trendy nightspots of the capital), but where were the Leinster fans when their team really needed them in Biarritz,

when victory would have guaranteed their progression to the knock-out stages? More than likely in Kiely's pub in Donnybrook, cursing their side's inadequacies before ordering another vodka and Red Bull.

The Munster fans who travelled in their thousands to Lille in 2001 were of an entirely different ilk. Not all of them were knowledgeable about rugby, many were GAA people who had never picked up an oval ball in their lives, but all were uniquely united in their appreciation of a wonderful team and their fierce pride in their province. A description of the scene in the residents' bar of a small hotel in Roubaix, some seven or eight hours after Stade Français and a shortsighted touch-judge had shattered Munster's dreams, provides a good example.

Festive cheer: the mighty Monsters roar on their team in Bordeaux.

There were maybe fifty Munster followers staying in a hotel seven miles outside Lille, and shortly after midnight we were all in the bar. Admittedly, at that hour, most were the worst for wear. In fact, some didn't seem too sure which European country they were in: 'Hey Amigo, any chance of a pint, boss? one man was overheard asking the harassed barman in a broad, if slightly slurred, Waterford accent. Every county in the province was represented, and as each group arrived back the soul-destroying events of the day were discussed again and again. The stories of people ringing home and hearing that television replays had proven conclusively that John O'Neill's try was legitimate only added to the sense of shared pain.

After a suitable amount of time had elapsed, a middle-aged gentleman from the Young Munster club in Limerick took control of proceedings. Brandishing an empty Pepsi bottle as a microphone, he called for hush. He then orchestrated a sing-song that made its way around the room. We had 'Limerick, You're a Lady' and 'My Lovely Rose of Clare'. Then a group from Tipperary sang 'Slievenamon'. Not be outdone, the large Cork contingent belted out 'The Banks of my own Lovely Lee', followed by the Kerry group doing their version of the 'Rose of Tralee'. Of course, we had the communal 'There is an Isle' and 'Beautiful, Beautiful Munsters', and an unrestrained 'Fields of Athenry' to wrap it all up. Everyone joined in, from children to those well into their sixties – a small gathering of people, representing an entire province, in a small town in northern France, hiding their disappointment behind a wall of song. Proudly singing for Munster. Doing Munster proud.

PETER STRINGER
BORN: 13/12/1977

In the 1999 World Cup, Ireland went into battle with Tom Tierney as first-choice scrum-half, yet Tierney was not even first choice for Munster. The red number nine jersey was in the possession of one 'Pistol' Peter Stringer – a 5ft 7ins, eleven stone gunslinger at the base of the scrum, firing bullets into the hands of his partner, Ronan O'Gara. However, Tierney is a fine player in his own right and his physical presence gave him the edge in the eyes of the Irish selectors. Even more intriguing was the presence of a third top-class scrum-half in Munster's squad. Cork Constitution's scrum-half Brian O'Meara had been capped back in 1997 and, like Tierney, would have been first choice at any of the other provinces, and yet he found himself third choice with Munster. So what did Declan Kidney value that the Irish selectors failed to purchase? In a word: passing.

In the modern game, any delay at the breakdown gives the opposition defence vital time to organise for the next attack, but Stringer gets the ball away immediately and this gives O'Gara vital seconds to make his play. Kidney had become convinced of Stringer's ability when he coached him at PBC, and though he knew O'Meara and Tierney were reliable players, when it came to a choice the Munster coach didn't hesitate. Stringer had played for Irish schools and had toured Australia in 1996. He went on to represent Irish Universities and the Ireland u21s, and was on the UCC side that won the European Students' Cup in 1999. The following season he joined Shannon as Munster's first-choice scrum-half, and his form was consistent and vital in Munster's progress through Europe.

Ireland had traditionally preferred combative scrum-halfs, men such as Michael Bradley, Niall Hogan and Tierney who could handle themselves in the tough environment that exists behind a beaten pack. When they eventually decided to opt for the quick service of Stringer, the diminutive Munsterman proved to be the key that unlocked a treasure chest of riches.

After Ireland's defeat at Twickenham, Stringer was called up to face Scotland and though, like fellow débutant O'Gara, he endured some tricky moments during the game, he emerged with reputation enhanced and firmly established as his country's first choice. Those who had doubted his ability to mix it with the big boys of the Six Nations were quickly put in their place. Ireland's captain Keith Wood admitted as much: 'I had no doubt about his ability, but his size was a different matter,' said Wood. 'I needn't have worried, he was exceptional.'

Stringer has been criticised for not posing enough of a threat with ball in hand, but to his credit he has introduced the sniping break into his game with some success. Additionally, when opposition runners have targetted Munster's slight number nine as an easy target, they have been surprised by his obdurate defence. It is a side to his game Stringer is very proud of. 'I love tackling, I love the physical side of the game,' he admits. However, it is passing that is Stringer's outstanding attribute, and the space he gives the men outside him has been absolutely crucial to Munster's success.

Munster's front-row of John Hayes, Frankie Sheahan and Peter Clohessy get ready to pack down against Biarritz in the European Cup quarter-final at Thomond Park in 2001.

CHAPTER SIX

RETREAT, REARM... RE-ENGAGE

How do you pick yourselves up again for another European campaign having lost out by a single point the previous season? It was not going to be easy. Ireland's tour of the Americas in the summer of 2000 certainly helped as the large Munster contingent in the squad were not afforded time to dwell on the painful defeat to Northampton. Declan Kidney was very conscious of the hangover from Twickenham and tried to give his players as much rest as possible before refocusing them for another assault on Europe. Ever the mind-doctor, Kidney also used the torture of Twickenham to motivate the squad and to cultivate a determination that this time they would go the distance. However, it was not a belief commonly held within rugby circles beyond the province.

Second season syndrome: the phenomenon whereby an individual or team fails to match the performance of the previous season due to increased levels of expectation. It was widely predicted for Munster in 2000/2001 as the European Cup hung in the balance once again. The element of surprise was gone, as were Keith Wood and Eddie Halvey, two of their most skilful and experienced operators. Wood had returned to Harlequins in London to fulfil his contract, while Halvey had decided to have a crack at professional rugby with Dick Best and London Irish. The general belief was that Munster had come so close to the summit, Kidney faced an extremely difficult task to motivate his men to begin the long,

John Kelly dispossesses Newport full-back Matt Pini during Munster's first European Cup clash of the 2000/2001 campaign at Thomond Park.

Frankie Sheahan goes over for the opening try against Newport at Thomond Park.

Former Springbok captain Gary Teichmann wins line-out possession for Newport against Munster. Teichmann admitted afterwards he was overcome by the atmosphere at Thomond Park.

tortuous ascent again. The majority of the squad and backroom team was the same, with John Langford staying on for another year, although Brian O'Brien's elevation to the job of Irish team manager led to the appointment of former coach Jerry Holland in what proved to be a seamless transition.

Newport, Castres and Bath: once again, Munster got a tough draw in what was unoriginally termed 'the group of death'. All three teams had money behind them and proud records at home, and there were wistful gazes in the direction of groups containing the weak Italian sides.

Munster's European campaign again kicked off at home to Welsh visitors as Newport made the journey to Thomond Park. This was an ambitious club and they had recruited a host of Southern Hemisphere stars in a bid to buy success. They were led by the Ex-Springbok captain Gary Teichmann, and he was joined by Adrian Garvey of Zimbabwe and South Africa, Matt Pini of Australia/Italy, Matt Mostyn of Australia/Ireland, Jason Jones-Hughes of Australia/Wales, and their playmaker, Shane Howarth, who

had represented both New Zealand and Wales (illegally as it turned out). The team had some Welsh players too, most notably second-row Ian Gough who had moved from Pontypridd.

Newport put it up to Munster, but once again Thomond Park witnessed a home victory as the Reds prevailed 26-18. Langford had been out for several weeks with a ligament injury, but came through well, and try-scorer Frankie Sheahan made a good start in his bid to prove wrong those who said the loss of Wood was catastrophic to the cause. Teichmann, who had seen it all in a long and distinguished career, was genuinely overcome by the atmosphere in the famous old ground. 'I couldn't get over how everyone stayed completely quiet for the kicks, it's something new to me', he said afterwards.

Munster were up and running again and off to a good start. The performances of Sheahan and Quinlan were of sufficient quality that the absence of Wood and Halvey was not really noticed. Next up was the trip to Castres, and though the events of the previous season had banished the

old fear with regard to the French, this was still a very difficult assignment. Like Toulouse the previous spring, revenge was on the cards for the older players as it was Castres who had sent Munster packing in the first year of the competition back in 1995/1996.

for Munster, and it was another one for the scrapbook. All-Black legend Gary Whetton was on holiday in France at the time and, having played for Castres in the early 1990s, he had gone to watch his old team in action. He left the stadium mightily impressed with the men from Munster.

The 2000 Castres vintage was captained by an Irishman, Jeremy Davidson, and one of his fellow 1997 Lions, the Scot Gregor Townsend, was at out-half. Like all French teams, Castres did not expect to be beaten at home and midway through the first-half the home side led by fourteen points. But Munster strengthened their resolve and by the 60th minute they had clawed their way back to parity. Castres responded in kind, and with time quickly running out they clung to a one-point lead at 26-25. Then Jason Holland, superb throughout, surged forward and instigated a clinching O'Gara try. The final score was 32-29

'It takes a really good team to beat Castres at home,' he said. 'Munster look like a quality side.'

Confidence among the team and the fans was high, and the visit of Bath to Thomond Park was an occasion to be savoured. Bath were the European club side of the 1990s, their success founded on good coaching and a strong West Country identity. They came to Limerick minus two of their biggest names – the English duo of Mike Catt and Jeremy Guscott – but a team-sheet containing the likes of Clarke, Regan, Borthwick, Lyle, Perry, Tindall, Balshaw and Maggs had to be taken very seriously. Bath arrived

Ronan O'Gara clears yet another hurdle as he retrieves the ball during Munster's training session in Castres.

convinced that they would be the ones to do what so many other teams had failed to do at Thomond Park, i.e., score more points than Munster. However, as all the others had found out, what sounds feasible in the quiet of hotel-room team meetings can prove impossible in the white heat of battle at a packed Thomond. The 31-9 final scoreline was every bit as resounding a defeat as it sounds. Anthony Foley bagged his customary man of the match award, while Anthony Horgan and John Kelly did much to dispel their 'unsung heroes' image. The only negative note was the line-out where Bath managed to disrupt the quality of possession.

The return match in Bath would produce an equally one-sided scoreline in favour of the home team. On a wet, miserable day at the Rec., Munster were never able to get going. The waterlogged pitch might have suited the old kick-and-chase Munster teams, but this side has always performed better on a dry sod. Their cause was not helped by the departure of their talisman, Mick Galwey, who left the field after only twenty-seven minutes because he had damaged his knee. Mick O'Driscoll gave his all when he came on, but the visitors missed the inspirational qualities of their captain. Once again, Bath dominated the line-out, thanks to the athleticism of Borthwick. Mike Catt ran the show for the home side and though they were unable to cross the try-line, their pressure tactics yielded eighteen points through the boot. Munster did score a try through

David Wallace, but there was no second-half resurgence, and they went into the long winter break knowing they had to beat Newport in Wales in the New Year to ensure their qualification for the knock-out stages.

They now faced a gap of over two months until the next European game in January. During this period Munster were crowned Interprovincial champions once again after securing a 16-16 draw with Leinster at Donnybrook. They were denied the Grand Slam, but had progressed through the competition unbeaten, emphasising their position as the best province in Ireland.

Then, in the middle of November, Ireland A defeated the touring Springboks 28-11 at Thomond Park. In the Irish line-up that night were Munstermen Mullins, Horgan, Staunton, Tierney, O'Driscoll, Quinlan and Wallace. All played their part in a superb team performance, with John Kelly doing his bit after coming on to replace Horgan. There was no doubt Kidney had a confident group of players at

Alone he stands: *coach Declan Kidney stands underneath the scoreboard deep into injury time against Castres.*

Going Dutch: *Jason Holland instigates another backline move against Castres.*

John Langford, with help from John Hayes, wins line-out possession during the win over Bath at Thomond Park.

his disposal, but he knew he would need another challenging outing before taking on Newport on their own patch. A friendly with Leinster was arranged for early January, and a sign of the times was that this 'friendly' fixture attracted 4,500 fans to Musgrave Park. This was no meaningless meeting: Leinster were out to prove a point as they were heartily sick of being constantly upstaged by their southern neighbours. The home side were dire in the first-half but improved subsequently, but Leinster were well worth their narrow win. Nonetheless, it was a worthwhile exercise and it would stand to Munster against Newport.

Munster v. Newport was the key battle of the group. Newport had to win to retain any hope of progressing. The match would be played in their Rodney Park ground, which had developed a reputation as something of a fortress, but Munster would not be without their support – over 3,000 fans made the journey to Wales. Injuries to Jason Holland and Mike Mullins meant an unusual centre pairing of John Kelly and Killian Keane, with big John O'Neill coming in on the wing.

The stadium was heaving, crammed full of Welshmen bedecked in the Newport colours and baying for blood. There was, however, a liberal sprinkling of red around the

ALAN QUINLAN
BORN: 13/7/1974

For many years it looked as though Alan Quinlan would never truly fulfil his potential. His talent was not in question, but his temperament most certainly was. Thankfully, that has all now changed and a more mature Quinlan has proven himself on both the provincial and international stages where his pace, hard tackling and line-out presence make him the prototype modern blindside flanker.

Originally from Clanwilliam in Tipperary, he joined Shannon as a youngster and his ready tongue quickly earned the nickname 'Cheeky'. A central part of the AIL-dominating Shannon side in the mid-1990s, he benefited from being part of a majestic back-row trio that included Anthony Foley and Eddie Halvey. Blessed with exceptional speed and a strong physique, Quinlan could play either openside or blindside, and was soon showcasing his talents in the red jersey.

A succession of brilliant displays in the European Cup during the 1997/1998 season attracted interest from Munster's pool opponents, Cardiff and Harlequins. Rumours abounded that the Shannonman was set to move across the Irish Sea, the trend for Irish internationals at the time, but Quinlan opted to stay put. The media generated a great deal of hype, believing an international call-up would be sooner rather than later, but selectors were not of the same opinion. At the time his game was still too inconsistent. Brilliant, eye-catching runs were not always matched by the kind of thankless gruntwork that marks the fully rounded player.

And then there was his self-discipline. Quinlan was not a man to back down and he harboured a fondness for 'sledging' the opposition. As a result, he attracted far too much attention from referees – a tendency not helped by an unfortunate peroxide period – and in the era of the sin-bin this was simply too costly at top level. Enter Declan Kidney who, with the help of Quinlan's club-mate Mick Galwey, taught the young flanker the benefits of self-control. His

performances improved accordingly, most notably one sensational display against Leinster at Donnybrook to secure another interprovincial trophy. In the 1999 World Cup against Romania, Quinlan finally won his first cap.

During Munster's march to the European Cup final, Quinlan was first choice at blindside until the knock-out stages. Then, a tactical switch by Kidney meant Quinlan lost out to Eddie Halvey for the game with Stade Français, and he also missed out on Bordeaux and Twickenham. The emergence of Llanelli's Simon Easterby saw him lose out at international level also, and it looked as though Quinlan might join the list of Ireland's one-cap wonders.

However, Halvey's departure for London Irish saw Quinlan re-establish himself in the Munster back-row. He excelled for Ireland A in the win over South Africa, and then a brilliant display in Munster's quarter-final against Biarritz in Thomond Park earned him an international recall for the Six Nations victories over Italy and France in 2001. Injury and the foot and mouth disease precautions ruined the rest of his season, but Quinlan is a quality player and still comparatively young so he should be around at the top level for years to come.

Who let the Claw out? *Peter Clohessy, with Frankie Sheahan and Mick Galwey in support, charges towards Bath's New Zealand out-half John Preston at Thomond Park.*

terraces and there was a splendid atmosphere by kick-off. Teichmann and his troops ran out determined to secure the victory they needed, and Munster were *blitzkrieged* as Newport raced into a 15-0 lead. Shane Howarth was dictating matters superbly from out-half and the intensity of the home side's forwards brooked no argument up front. At this point the game looked like a done deal. Each Newport score was greeted by a chorus of 'Who let the dogs out?' booming out over the PA system, and everywhere there was black-and-yellow delirium. Tom Mulqueen, one of Munster's most loyal fans, takes up the story: 'We were down 15-0. This was not good and the Welsh supporters had us written off, and if they had got one more score they might have been right, but then Munster slowly started to get to grips with the match. They got to the Newport 25 and it was the first time they'd gotten this close to the line, and I remember a frantic voice called out from the crowd "for F**** sake, sing will ye!", as if that was going to solve all our problems. The crowd duly obliged and it seemed to work because next minute Ronan

O'Gara got a very precious try and Munster went in at half-time trailing by 21-10.'

A full weekend of All-Ireland League fixtures meant a lot of Munster fans were unable to travel due to club commitments, including yours truly. Listening to the match on the radio in a minibus somewhere between Ballinahinch and Dublin was at first nerve-wracking and then spine-tingling. From what seemed an impossible position, Munster began to fight back, with Ronan O'Gara giving a *tour de force* display. The young Corkman contributed a try, two drop-goals, four penalties and three conversions. The crucial score came midway through the second-half when Mike Mullins, who had come on as a substitute, left the Newport defenders stranded as he scorched through to touchdown. That was the watershed.

Once Munster got going they were unstoppable, and the fans loved it. As things began to turn in their favour, the supporters began chanting 'Who let the Claw out?', a delicious response to Newport's earlier triumphalism. By the time Anthony Horgan intercepted to run the length of the field and score under the posts, it was all over: 39-24 and we had yet another unforgettable Munster occasion. It also provided a 'Where were you when?' moment, and that bumpy bus-ride from Ballinahinch will never be forgotten by those who experienced it.

Qualification had been secured, but there was still a huge scramble for tickets when Castres arrived on another wet and miserable day at Musgrave Park. Munster produced another professional, workmanlike performance to run out 21-11 winners, with Foley scoring the crucial try and his back-row colleague, David Wallace, taking the man of the match accolade. The game marked the return to action of Jason Holland who came on at half-time and acquitted himself well in the second-half.

That day also provided the eeriest moment I have ever experienced at a Munster match. During a break in play the supporters began singing 'The Fields of Athenry', but not in the usual loud, raucous manner. Instead they sang quietly, almost conversationally. There was nothing really to get too excited about that grey day in Muzzer, but the rain-drenched fans wanted to offer their appreciation to the team that had given them so much pleasure. People sitting in the stands later recounted how, peering through

A delighted David Wallace slips over under the posts to score a try against Bath at Thomond Park.

Peter Stringer *employs the old-fashioned dive pass to get the ball away against Leinster during a specially arranged warm-up match. The 'friendly' fixture still attracted a huge crowd to Musgrave Park.*

the mist, they gradually became aware of this haunting song rising from the terraces all around them. As they finished the final chorus, the supporters broke into applause and it felt as if they were applauding themselves as much as the team. It was a wonderfully surreal moment.

The quarter-final the following weekend saw Biarritz, who had qualified from Leinster's pool, bidding to banish the aura of invincibility that pervaded Thomond Park. Earlier in the season they had been destroyed by Leinster in Donnybrook, and although they subsequently improved tenfold, it was hard to dampen the ardour of the optimists who were convinced that the Frenchmen faded when taken away from their home comforts. The more knowledgeable were not fooled. Their right-wing, Philippe Bernat-Salle (incidentally, a dead-ringer for Richard Chamberlain in *The*

Count of Monte Cristo), was one the world's deadliest finishers. Frano Botica, the veteran Kiwi who had enjoyed successful careers in league and union, was their canny general at out-half, while up front they could draw on the vast experience of French internationals Jean Michel Gonzalez and Olivier Roumat. Indeed, the forward unit was so strong they could afford to leave the Lievremonts on the bench, although there was no doubt they would feature at some stage.

Munster welcomed Holland back into the starting line-up and the players took the field full of confidence and wearing their rather fetching change strip to avoid a clash with the red of Biarritz. The home side took advantage of every break that came their way in the first-half, and by the 65th minute they had built up a commanding 32-15 lead. That man Foley was on fire once again and crashed over for three tries. The Thomond faithful were lapping it up, busy dialling their twenty-four-hour banking numbers to ready funds for the semi-final. Then, without warning, Biarritz woke up. Concerted forward drives and imaginative back play yielded a succession of scores and left Munster reeling. With the home fans willing the game to end and the score at 35-29, the chanting for Munster carried with it more than a hint of concern. Kidney showed his customary reluctance to make substitutions, and with Biarritz pushing for a winning score we wondered if the fifteen heroes in red could hold on.

In injury time, Munster were awarded a penalty from the half-way line. O'Gara, cool as a breeze, indicated his preference for a shot at goal. Good decision, we thought approvingly, run down the clock. Then, as Arthur Daley might put it: 'Wot appens? The geezer only goes an' slots it! Straight up .... from the 'arfway line .... the job was oxo, mate.' But it was a close-run thing. Biarritz had shown what

*Leinster's **Bob Casey** runs into Anthony Foley with the supporting Malcolm O'Kelly outnumbered by the Munster heavies: John Langford, Gaillimh, the Claw and John 'The Bull' Hayes.*

Killian Keane gets the ball away during the famous win over Newport at Rodney Parade.

a good side they were and one could only speculate what would have happened had they woken up a bit earlier. Nevertheless, despite their stuttering performance in the second-half, Munster deserved to make the semi-finals. Ironically, having won the award so often in the past, Foley didn't get man of the match on the day he had scored three tries, instead that honour went to Alan Quinlan who had produced a superb all-round display.

The three other teams remaining in the competition were Leicester and Gloucester of England, together with Munster's old adversaries, Stade Français. The significance of Munster's achievement in reaching the semi-finals was emphasised by the fact that they were the only one of the previous season's semi-finalists to repeat the feat. Title-holders Northampton had endured an abject campaign, winning only one group match, while Toulouse failed to

reach the last eight for the first time having lost to Cardiff and Saracens and being held to a draw by Ulster.

Following the customary break for the Six Nations, the draw for the European Cup semi-finals was announced. The entire province went down on bended knee to pray that we would get Gloucester out of the hat. However, just like the previous season, Munster got the short straw – away to Stade Français, the outstanding team in the competition so far. You could see Declan Kidney desperately trying to put on a brave face, but inside he must have been wondering what he had done to offend the Almighty. Conspiracy theorists were convinced it was part of the organisers' grand plan for an Anglo-French, Leicester–Stade finale.

Munster's luck did not improve. The foot and mouth crisis meant all play was cancelled in Ireland, and then, as the 21 April semi-final date loomed, the team was hit by an injury crisis. Quinlan was definitely out, as was winger John Kelly. Wallace was considered extremely doubtful and Stringer, Crotty and Foley had all suffered injury in the previous month and had questionmarks hanging over them. But Munster's all-Ireland back-row was the biggest headache. Foley, Wallace and Quinlan had started all seven of Munster's European games that season, and had only twice failed to finish as a unit when Colm McMahon got brief cameos in the games against Bath.

A warm-up game against a Rest of Ireland XV in Thomond Park was arranged, and served a two-fold purpose: to give Munster much-needed match practice ahead of the Stade challenge, and, having been denied the usual stage of the Six Nations by foot and mouth, to provide an opportunity for Ireland's contenders to strut their stuff in front of the watching Lions coach Graham Henry. This game was notable for the appearance of former Irish captain Dion O'Cuinneagain in the Munster jersey. When Kidney had selected O'Cuinneagain as one of the two additions to his European Cup squad there was widespread surprise, especially as the dental student was studying in his native South Africa. However, injuries to Dave Wallace and Alan Quinlan necessitated a call-up and once again the extraordinary foresightedness of the Munster coach was

Munster out-half *Ronan O'Gara tries an inside break against opposite number Shane Howarth, as John O'Neill supports during the win over Newport at Rodney Parade.*

Ronan O'Gara slices through the Castres defence on a wet and misty day at Musgrave Park.

illustrated. O'Cuinneagain was barely off the plane, but did quite well when he came on in the match, which was played before a packed house. Munster encouragingly won 24-22. While the win was welcome, preparations at this stage were far from ideal.

As it transpired, Foley and Wallace had been pencilled in to start in the match against Stade, but Kidney needed someone to fill Quinlan's influential role at blindside. O'Cuinneagain would represent a huge gamble, given his lack of match practice and his lack of familiarity with the squad, so the coach turned to Donncha O'Callaghan, the versatile youngster from Cork Constitution. O'Callaghan was primarily a second-row, but he had a lot of experience of the back-row and, at 6ft 6ins and seventeen stone, was certainly physically equipped for the task. However, this was some game in which to make your first European Cup start and it remained to be seen if he could handle the intense pressure. Filling John Kelly's spot on the wing was

more straightforward as John O'Neill had proven in the past that he was up to the job and had the necessary big-match temperament. Kidney's response to the injury crisis was typically upbeat. 'You always regret injuries from the perspective of the injured party,' he said, 'but you have to look at it as a great opportunity for the guys coming in.'

The noises coming from Paris suggested Stade were in trouble too. They had their own injury problems, were tired from a long season and in their last game lost to Castres, although Diego Dominguez had still managed to kick twenty-nine points. Christophe Dominici, their electric winger/full-back, declared that, in his eyes, Munster were favourite for the title – proving that the French knew how to play mind-games with the best of them.

DOMINIC CROTTY

BORN: 28/7/1974

When Dominic Crotty was injured against Leinster in 1999 he lost his place on the Munster team, and by the time he had recovered, Jeremy Staunton had nailed down the full-back position. Then the 44-strong Irish panel for the upcoming Six Nations and A Championships was announced and, despite the presence of sixteen Munstermen, there was no place for Crotty. Yet what followed was the most remarkable period in the young Corkman's career.

First he won his Munster place back, and starred as they scorched their way to the European Cup final. He then played a vital role in the championship-winning Ireland A team, received a recall to the full national colours on Ireland's tour to the Americas and, to cap it all, married fiancée Karen O'Leary on his return.

Educated at CBC, Crotty comes from a family steeped in sporting heritage and it was no surprise when he showed great promise at tennis and rugby. When he left school he joined UCC and became an automatic choice for the university rugby team at the tender age of seventeen. Crotty was regularly appearing on 'One to Watch' lists as he ran in tries for the Cork college from all over the park.

Combining footballing intelligence, deceptive speed and a strong physique, Crotty had all the qualities needed in an attacking full-back. However, when his first cap came against Australia in 1996 the selectors, in their infinite wisdom, placed him on the wing. Lacking the searing pace of a genuine winger, Crotty used his footballing ability to survive that day, but he still looked far more comfortable when moved to full-back following an injury to Jim Staples. He was kept on the wing for the next two internationals against Italy and France, but then against Wales, Ieuan Evans, one of the world's best wingers, gave him a roasting. The selectors wielded the axe and Crotty retreated to his lair to lick his wounds.

In truth, it took him two years to get over the effect that day at the Cardiff Arms Park had on his confidence, but the faith shown in him by Declan Kidney played a huge part in restoring his self-belief.

Fast forward to December 1999 and Crotty, fully recovered from injury, comes on as a substitute against Colomiers at Musgrave Park to score a memorable try in the corner. Putting aside his omission from the Irish set-up, he knuckled down and won his Munster place back. By the time of the Stade Français quarter-final the Garryowen player was on a roll. A succession of injuries had seen him called into the Ireland A side where he proved he had what it takes to survive at international level, and at Thomond Park against Stade he was simply outstanding. His international recall against Canada that summer was no less than he deserved.

Crotty has been the model of consistency at full-back for Munster, mixing solid defence with attacking adventurousness, and he can be proud of the role he has played.

Gaillimh leads out *Munster in their change strip for the European Cup quarter-final against Biarritz at Thomond Park.*

Meanwhile, more than 10,000 match-starved Munster fans had made arrangements to travel to support their team. The game would be played in Lille, an industrial city in northeast France, close to the Belgian border. It was a strange choice of venue as Lille had no rugby pedigree and was primarily a soccer town. Some fans elected to fly in and out on the day, others were planning to head to London and get the Eurostar train to Brussels and transfer to Lille, while more decided to base themselves in Brussels for the weekend. Our particular group spurned the easy options and elected to drive to Rosslare, catch the overnight ferry to Cherbourg and then drive along the north coast of France to Roubaix, a small town just outside Lille. On paper (once again) it looked great, but in reality, like everything else that weekend, it proved to be extremely trying. On the Thursday before the match, 500 Munster fans poured onto the ferry and were greeted by a bewildered staff totally unprepared for the onslaught. Supporters don't expect much on these trips – easy access to the bar and a sing-song would suffice. Instead, the bar was six-deep all night with a handful of unfortunate barmen run off their feet. 'We didn't know there was a

Little and Large: *Peter Stringer goes head-to-head with the kneeling Biarritz prop Emmanuel Menieu during the European Cup quarter-final at Thomond Park.*

bleedin' match on,' was their repeated wail. Strange that, since the ferry tickets were all pre-booked. A trip to the bar took up to twenty-five minutes, and as soon as you got back you had to return for more as frustration tends to encourage an awful thirst. On top of that, the onboard entertainment was of *The Loveboat* variety. As knees-ups go it was pretty dire, and even the requested 'Fields of Athenry' failed to hit the right note. The murdering of the Munster anthem and the continued absence of alcohol necessitated a swift conference and an equally swift retreat to the cot.

The following day, things did not improve. The drive to Roubaix, which looked so easy on the map, turned out to be excessively long and monotonous. It took seven hours in all, alleviated only by a couple of motorway stops and a poignant journey through the Somme battlefield and various First World War cemeteries. Finally we reached Roubaix, a gorgeous little town just outside Lille, and the mood improved as the pre-match atmosphere began to build among the many fans present.

21 April 2001: match day dawned cold and blustery, and gazing at the grey sky we wondered what the afternoon would bring. Lille town centre seemed as ill-equipped to cope with the Munster onslaught as the ferry had been. The pubs were overcrowded and all were complaining of a shortage of glasses, so the vast majority of fans arrived at the stadium in an unaccustomed state of sobriety. (That is not, of course, to suggest that Munster fans are a collection of drunkards, but a few pints definitely heightens the emotions and thereby one's quality of support.) Certainly, it was all a far cry from Twickenham eleven months earlier; we arrived at the stadium, a persistent drizzle leaving us damp in spirit and body. Unfortunately, the stadium itself was not designed to lift one's mood: cold, concrete and cheerless.

There were distractions, however. Familiar faces were greeted excitedly and famous faces were pointed out in the crowd. Pat Shortt of D'Unbelievables was spotted, as was Ireland coach Warren Gatland, and one had to feel sympathy for Fine Gael leader Michael Noonan who got an

Anthony Foley crashes over for one of his three tries against Biarritz, but his performance still couldn't get him the man of the match award ahead of Alan Quinlan.

John O'Neill troubled the Stade Français defence all afternoon in Lille. Here the winger makes yet another powerful burst during his man of the match performance.

unmerciful going-over (verbally) when he went to the Gents. It seemed to be predominantly Munster fans present, but when we took our place behind the goalposts we could see the Stade fans congregated solemnly at the far end. A look through the programme reinforced the impression that Munster had a massive challenge on their hands. As well as their best weapon, Dominguez, Stade had the gritty number eight Juillet, the promising young lock Auredou partnered by the giant Canadian James, and the uncompromising South African/Frenchman De Villiers at prop. In the backs they had the beautifully coiffured Morgan 'Kajagoogoo' Williams at scrum-half, and the combined forces of Comba, Lombard and Dominici out wide. The long lay-off and injury problems were always going to make a good outcome difficult, but opposition of this quality made it doubly so. To top it all, the cheerless day had become bitterly cold and wet, and the distance of the fans from the field made it almost impossible to generate any atmosphere. The stadium was simply not suitable for a European Cup semi-final: the quality of the pitch, the Iron Curtain architecture and the malfunctioning scoreboard all added up to a pretty shoddy display.

The game got underway and Stade Français immediately went on the offensive. Munster looked out of sorts. The communication between Frankie Sheahan and his jumpers was garbled and Munster were starved of possession as a result. Young O'Callaghan had a difficult start, knocking on an early ball, and he looked unnerved by the importance of the occasion. To his credit he knuckled down and improved as the game wore on, but there was no doubt that Quinlan's experience was missed. Wallace was clearly struggling too. We were so accustomed to his routine excellence that to see the number seven so off the pace

The match-starved Monsters travelled in their thousands to France for the European Cup semi-final. The fans pose for the camera in Lille town centre before the clash with Stade Français.

was particularly disturbing. He was obviously carrying his injury and Stade were profiting as a result. Munster's defence seemed to be holding, but in attack they looked slow and predictable. Mullins and Holland were well-marshalled by their opposite numbers, and only John O'Neill seemed to represent a threat when the ball went wide. The big man looked as though he were dying to get involved and ran hard and aggressively at every opportunity. After a flurry of penalties, Stade grabbed the first try – ironically, from a backline move they called 'Munster'. The livewire scrum-half 'Kajagoogoo' sliced through and a sweeping move ended with veteran Kiwi Cliff Mytton diving over the touchline.

At half-time the mood among the fans was despondent. It was hard to see where a Munster try would come from, and Stade, with Dominici threatening every time he touched the ball, were far more imaginative with their possession. Nonetheless, we had been in this position before and fought our way back, so as the teams ran out for the second-half the chants went up again with renewed urgency. And the men in red responded.

The Claw and Gaillimh took up the challenge and began charging at the opposition, while O'Neill took up

where he had left off in the first-half. The game's critical moment came in the 52nd minute when O'Gara sent a perfectly judged cross-field kick into the right corner. O'Neill raced onto it, gathered it and crashed over the line. Situated directly behind that corner the initial impression from the blur of bodies and flagpost was that it was a no-try. However, we were used to the use of video referees in the Six Nations, so we waited expectantly for the referee to make a rectangular shape with his hands. It never happened. Apparently, a game of this importance – one which was being beamed around Europe and had tempted 10,000 Munster fans to journey to this grey northeast corner of France – did not warrant the use of video technology. The referee signalled no-try to the sound of tortured groans from the red faithful. Munster redoubled their efforts.

Ronan O'Gara kicked fifteen points that afternoon, but it was his 'missed kick' in the 67th minute that provoked the most comment. Again, we were positioned perfectly

The picture that broke 10,000 hearts: Irish Examiner *photographer Dan Linehan proves conclusively that John O'Neill's try should have stood and Munster should have reached their second European Cup final.*

behind the posts, in line with the flight of the ball, and red arms were thrust aloft as the ball clearly travelled inside the posts. But after hesitation and worried glances, the touch-judges inexplicably decided to keep their flags lowered. This was just too much. Kidney sent on O'Cuinneagain and we waited expectantly for the South African to break free on one of his trademark sprints. It never happened, and the clock ticked down inexorably towards disaster.

It was now a one-point game, 16-15, and a distinct feeling of *déjà vu* came over all of us who had been at Twickenham the previous year. Not again, oh God no, not again. The whistle blows. An awful feeling washes over you. Everything inside screams, 'Get out, get away from this horrible, cold, wet place where we have been so wronged.' But no one moved. We were transfixed. Forced to watch as the gaudy colours of the Stade supporters bobbed all over the stadium.

We had to stay because we knew the team would come over to us. There was no bitterness towards the players. Once again they had given their all and nobody could ask for more than that. Kidney led them over on the slowest lap ever seen on the Lille running-track. The players were quite obviously distraught, we were distraught, it was awful. Langford had his arms around Kidney, tears streaming freely down his cheeks – he had just played what he thought was his last game for Munster. He was not the only one crying. It was completely understandable, everything had conspired against them – foot and mouth disease, injuries, the away draw, the officials – and despite all of that it had once again come down to a single point. To heighten the misery, the heavens now really opened, and as we huddled together wordlessly, wet through and thoroughly miserable, news started to filter back via various mobile phone-users that television replays had proven conclusively that O'Neill's try was valid, as was O'Gara's penalty kick. We were gutted.

In the aftermath, Munster captain Mick Galwey spoke candidly about the hurt they all experienced. 'It would have been better if we got a hiding. It's tough to lose, but worse when you know a bad call was responsible.' Kidney, typically, refused to point the finger at the officials. Even

Coach Declan Kidney *tries to put on a brave face in Lille, but John Langford breaks down after what he thought, at the time, was his last match for Munster.*

looking back a few months later he remains sanguine. 'There's three things in every game you have to consider: the weather, the referee and yourselves. You have no control over the weather and the referee, so we have to ask ourselves, did we do enough to win that day?'

Kidney's restraint was admirable, but as supporters the overwhelming feeling was one of bitterness. To have come so far, against all the odds, and to be denied in such a high-profile game by official incompetence and technological inadequacy was sheer torture. We could no longer take solace in good performance and worthy defeat. This team and their supporters deserved more. They deserved a European Cup.

A clearly devastated *Anthony Horgan, Donncha O'Callaghan, Mick Galwey, Ronan O'Gara, Dominic Crotty and Peter Stringer embark on a slow lap of the Lille stadium.*

RED TO GREEN –

CHAPTER SEVEN

Stade de France, March 2000:
Ireland celebrate their first win over
France in Paris since 1972. Munster
players Peter Stringer, Keith Wood,
Mike Mullins, Peter Clohessy and
John Hayes are to the fore.

GO!

'*Fifty reasons to get radical.'* **The Monday morning headline in the** *Irish Examiner* **said it all – Ireland had just suffered the humiliation of a 50-18 hammering by the old enemy England at Twickenham. Heading into the game with high hopes, the Irish team had been totally overwhelmed by Clive Woodward's men, and got their Six Nations campaign off to the worst possible start. If that was not bad enough, following the game there was an incident involving reserve hooker Frankie Sheahan at a Kensington hotel, in which the Munsterman was alleged to have headbutted an irate supporter. All very unsavoury, and coming just a few months after Ireland's ignominious exit to Argentina in the World Cup, it seemed as though we had sunk to an all-time low.**

In fact, the entire 1990s had been a disaster for the Irish rugby team. Throughout the decade we were constantly getting whacked with the Five Nations' wooden spoon. Ireland had not beaten Scotland, whose rugby-playing population was of a similar size to our own, since 1988 – a truly horrifying statistic. We had not beaten France since 1983, and regular humiliations were suffered in Paris where Ireland's last victory was back when Jesus was a carpenter, or 1972 to be precise. England had been stunned in 1993 and 1994, but had gone on to exact revenge with ruthless regularity. It was only against Wales, and, more remarkably, in Cardiff, that we ever had any moments of joy.

So as the new millennium dawned, Irish rugby sought to put the dark days of the 1990s behind and begin a bright new era – only to see it all go pear-shaped at the first time of asking. The Irish team that day at Twickers was simply swatted away. There was a silver lining from a Munster point of view, however. Anthony Foley, back in the international side after a three-year absence, got through a tremendous amount of work and did more than enough to justify his recall. Additionally, Mick Galwey, omitted in favour of the hopelessly out-of-depth Robert Casey, was belatedly called into the side at half-time and managed to organise at least some semblance of resistance in the green ranks. There is no doubt that Galwey's experience prevented the scoreline from reaching even more embarrassing proportions, and he even chipped in with a try on what was his twenty-fifth international appearance.

In the fall-out from Twickenham there was a massive clamouring for change. It appeared the Irish rugby-loving public had had enough. Why couldn't we emulate our provincial success in the international arena? The game had been professional for five years, our players were earning big money to represent their country and it really was high time for some return on investment. Warren Gatland and his management team decided something

drastic had to be done, and for the Scottish game five new caps were introduced. Along with Simon Easterby and Shane Horgan, first caps were handed to Munstermen: Ronan O'Gara, Peter Stringer and John Hayes. This was a deliberate attempt by Gatland to transfer the self-belief, doggedness and will-to-win of Declan Kidney's Munster to the national side. To the delight of his many admirers, Gaillimh was also given a

The five new caps brought in by the Irish selectors for the Scotland game after the embarrassing loss to England. Peter Stringer, Ronan O'Gara and John Hayes of Munster made their débuts alongside Shane Horgan of Leinster (front left) and Simon Easterby of Llanelli.

long overdue recall to the starting fifteen. Not only was this recognition of the fine rugby he was playing, it was also a prudent move by the selectors who knew the presence of the big man from Currow would do much to ease the nerves of Munster's young débutants.

The biggest surprise was the selection of John Hayes over Paul Wallace. Wallace had been viewed as practically infallible since his barn-storming displays for the Lions in South Africa in 1997. He had been an automatic choice for Ireland ever since that tour, whereas Hayes had been spoken of as promising but still too raw for the tough environment of international rugby. But recently Wallace had been struggling to cope with the challenge of Julian White at his club, Saracens, and was frequently criticised for giving away too many penalties. So the selectors were now prepared to take a gamble on the big Shannonman. Although Hayes's work-rate was exemplary, concern was expressed that his scrummaging was suspect. Against

You've been Munstered: Peter Clohessy, Anthony Foley and John Hayes tear into the Scottish forwards during the international at Lansdowne Road in 2000.

Scotland he would be up against another Lion, the doughty Tom Smith, and there would be no room for error. The pressure was on Hayes to prove his mettle.

There were now eight members of the Munster team in the fifteen to face Scotland, including the entire front-row and both half-backs. The Scots had not lost to Ireland for twelve years, and we wondered whether the introduction of the Munster factor could possibly be enough to give Ireland the victory we all craved. The answer was an emphatic Yes. The Scots weren't just beaten, they were stuffed. Munster and co. racked up an impressive 44-22 scoreline, and the tide – the red tide – had turned for Ireland.

All the Munstermen performed well, and Hayes, in particular, had an outstanding début, silencing the doubters. He coped well with the slippery Smith, and put in a huge performance around the field. Both Stringer and O'Gara struggled at times with the step-up, but, to their credit, they persevered and came through with their reputations bolstered. The Irish showed a new confidence that day, borne out of the fact that the Munster players were used to winning and refused to panic when things went against them. Galwey's influence was immense. He made it his business to calm the youngsters' nerves before kick-off, throwing his arms around the young half-backs O'Gara and Stringer during the singing of the national anthem.

The new sense of self-belief was evident in the subsequent victories over Italy, and especially in Paris in our first win over France in twenty-eight years. The speed of passing from Stringer gave O'Gara time to pull the strings at out-half, and for the first time in years the Irish backline looked genuinely threatening. The up-and-coming Brian O'Driscoll now had the time and space he needed to wreak havoc, and he gorged upon it greedily, famously scoring three tries.

A major factor in the revitalising of the Irish Senior team was the success of the A side. Here again, the Munster factor was much in evidence as Declan Kidney and Niall O'Donovan were in control of the second stringers. Self-belief was vital, and there were several eleventh-hour victories as Ireland captured the Six Nations A Championship.

Irish scrum-half *Peter Stringer celebrates with Anthony Foley and Kevin Maggs after the epic win over France in Paris in 2000.*

The Bull charges past French second-row Fabien Pelous in the 2001 Six Nations game at Lansdowne Road.

Ireland's captain Keith Wood charges for the line with Wales' scrum-half Rupert Moon trying desperately to hang on at Lansdowne Road in 2000.

ANTHONY HORGAN

BORN: 15/11/1976

When Tyrone Howe was called out to join the Lions in Australia in June 2001, many rugby supporters in Munster felt it could have been Anthony Horgan travelling had the Irish selectors given him the recognition he deserved. When Ireland turned to Munster practically en bloc after the humiliation in Twickenham, Horgan was one of the few left out in the cold. And despite his consistently excellent form for Munster in defence and attack, Howe was subsequently chosen ahead of him the following season. The feeling down south was that the selectors were making a concession to Ulster by picking Howe, as the province would otherwise have had no representative on the national team.

Whereas Horgan did not get many opportunities to express himself in attack during Munster's march to the European final in 2000, the following season he prospered as the ball became a more frequent visitor to his left-hand touchline. The seventy-yard breakaway try in Newport might stick in the memory, but it was Horgan's earlier performance against Bath at Thomond Park that marked him out as a performer of true international quality. His opponent that day was England's boy wonder Iain Balshaw, and Horgan won the contest with ease, notching up two tries and looking assured in defence throughout. There is no longer any question about his ability, the one remaining doubt concerns his facility for picking up injuries, which has hampered his progress.

A product of PBC, Horgan came under the guidance of Declan Kidney in school, and the Munster coach was always convinced of his all-round quality. He joined Cork Constitution after leaving school and was on the team that won the 1999 All-Ireland League title.

Although he does not conform to the trend of giant wingers – in place since the 6ft 5ins, nineteen stone Jonah Lomu emerged in 1995 – Horgan is a tenacious tackler and is rarely bested by his opposite number. Then there is his pace, this guy is a genuine speedster and can augment it with an ability to swerve and jink at full tilt. Kidney has always been a huge fan of his flame-haired winger's talents and, except when he was unavailable due to injury, he has been an ever-present figure in Kidney's Munster sides.

Although he has willingly embraced professional rugby and all its regimes, Horgan, thankfully, does not live for the game alone and is known for his ability to enjoy himself off the pitch, a trait reflected in his enthusiastic play on it.

Whether or not we have banished the bad old days remains to be seen. After the *joie de vivre* of Paris, Wales took the rug out from under Ireland by inflicting a surprise defeat at Lansdowne Road. A subsequent loss to Argentina, followed by a less-than-impressive display against Canada (and against Romania the following year) suggest that we still struggle to motivate ourselves against the so-called lesser nations. However, a stirring performance against South Africa in Lansdowne Road in the autumn of 2000, followed by victories over Italy and France in the disrupted 2001 Six Nations, indicated that the encouraging revival of the previous season was no flash in the pan. The Irish pack in that 2001 campaign read as follows: Clohessy, Wood, Hayes, Galwey, O'Kelly, Quinlan, Foley and Wallace. Only Malcolm O'Kelly could claim no link with Munster, and the selection of the Munster forwards practically *en bloc* was vindicated by those back-to-back victories in the Six Nations. The emergence of Quinlan and Wallace as first-choice flankers was not before time. Quinlan was now a more rounded player than the flamboyant but undisciplined performer he had been a few years previously, while Wallace's consistent excellence simply had to be recognised at national level.

There is absolutely no doubt that the cancellation of matches due to foot and mouth disease affected Ireland's representation on the Lions tour. Certainly two Munstermen, Wallace and Hayes, had reason to be most aggrieved by their non-selection. Despite an average Six Nations campaign, Wales had ten men in the original Lions squad, including openside Martyn Williams and tight-head prop David Young. Williams had been reasonable for Wales, whereas Wallace had been inspirational for Ireland and Munster all season. The Garryowen man had looked the best ball-carrying back-row in the championship and, foot and mouth disease notwithstanding, fully deserved a seat on the plane to Australia. As it transpired, Wallace would receive a call-up after Lawrence Dallaglio's tour was ended prematurely by injury, but the fact remains that he should have been on the plane in the first instance.

A right pair: proud Munster warriors Peter Clohessy and Mick Galwey get ready to do battle for their country. Both men successfully reinvented themselves with Ireland when nearing the end of their careers.

During the 2001 Six Nations
Championship, David Wallace proved to
the rugby world what Munster supporters
already knew: he is world-class.

Similarly to Williams, Young had done nothing spectacular that season, or indeed in his whole career. The veteran Welshman had a reputation as a punishing scrummager that was not deserved. His stint as Welsh captain had been less than successful and his contribution away from the set-piece was negligible. In short, Young seemed to be trading on his name and the fact that he had toured with the Lions twelve years previously. Hayes, by comparison, continued to excel for province and country. Commentators constantly questioned his scrummaging, but there is no way the teams he soldiered for could have enjoyed as much success as they did if he were deficient in that crucial department. Hayes would have been a roaring success for the Lions in Australia.

Instead, Munster had to be content with one Lion – Ronan O'Gara – or three if you count Keith Wood and Rob Henderson. (Henderson signed for the province shortly before the tour began.) O'Gara's selection was entirely on merit, despite allegations from Gregor Townsend supporters that Lions' manager Donal Lenihan had swung the vote in favour of his Cork Constitution club-mate. The simple fact was that Ronan had impressed the Lions' selectors with his accomplished displays for Ireland and Munster over the previous two seasons, and his goal-kicking excellence gave him the edge over Townsend who had endured a poor season with Scotland. O'Gara's ascent reflects the new confidence in Irish rugby, a new belief that is, touch wood, here to stay.

Of course, this is not all down to Munster and it would be wrong to claim as much. The emergence of talented players, such as Brian O'Driscoll and Shane Horgan, and the good structure put in place by the IRFU have all contributed. However, the Munster factor cannot be discounted. Young players weaned on the cannyness of Kidney and Galwey, and taught the simple doctrine that it is never over until the large female begins to trill, have wrought a change in Irish rugby that is, hopefully, irreversible.

Ronan O'Gara gets the Irish backline moving during the win over Italy in Rome in 2001.

O'Gara celebrates scoring a try for his country against Italy in Rome.

Looking at the young talent in Declan Kidney's squad it is hard to quell the overwhelming feeling of optimism. Players like Jeremy Staunton, Marcus Horan, Mick O'Driscoll, Conor Mahony and Donncha O'Callaghan can step in and take this team forward when the elder lemons lapse into richly deserved retirement. Even more encouraging, established stars like Peter Stringer, Ronan O'Gara, David Wallace and Anthony Horgan are only in their mid-20s and have years of top-class rugby left in them, which can only be good for Munster, and for Ireland.

The future looks bright, the future looks red.

JOHN KELLY
BORN: 18/4/1974

Cork Constitution's John Kelly is Declan Kidney's ideal player. He may have been left behind when Munster's success led to a host of call-ups to the national side, but Kelly has always been one of the first names on Kidney's team-sheet. A footballer of consummate skill, Kelly is another of Munster's players whose excellence lies in the absence of error in his game.

Unlike many of his Cork team-mates he did not go to either of the rugby nurseries of PBC or CBC, instead attending Rochestown College. Although not a recognised rugby school, Rochestown has produced internationals in Darragh O'Mahoney and David Corkery who, like Kelly, played their juvenile rugby at Cork Constitution. On leaving school, Kelly went to UCC and received numerous caps for the Irish Universities, including the Test match on the tour to Australia in 1997. It was no surprise when Kelly rejoined Con. following his graduation, and when Declan Kidney took over as Munster coach, Kelly gradually began to establish himself in the Munster squad. His good form was reflected in an appearance for the Combined Provinces against the touring South Africans in 1998, but one feels he might have made a better impression if he had been lining out in the red of Munster instead of being part of a cobbled-together side.

When Munster began their great run in 1999/2000, Kelly was an important member of the team. He admits himself there was surprise expressed at his elevation to the Munster team because public perception was that Kelly really was no more than a competent club player. 'I'm probably seen as a player who doesn't do that much wrong, but nothing particularly brilliant either,' he said. However, his role in Munster's progress was reflected in his promotion to the highly successful A side that season, where he distinguished himself once again.

Kidney has used Kelly's footballing abilities on the wing and at outside-centre, and he looks comfortable in both positions. Though not blessed with blinding pace, Kelly is nonetheless deceptively quick and has the ability to change direction at full tilt. Positioned at centre, his forty-metre run through the centre of Newport's defence at Rodney Parade is a stand-out memory from a series of accomplished performances.

Kelly's greatest qualities are his intelligent defending and his innate footballing abilities. Unfortunately, the presence of a certain Brian O'Driscoll will limit his chances of demonstrating his talents in the Ireland number thirteen shirt, and he is unlikely to get a shot on the wing at the highest level. However, as Kelly has progressed up the proverbial ladder since his days at Rochestown College he has excelled at each successive rung, particularly in the red of Munster. Should a full cap ever materialise, you would back him to once again prove his worth.

SEASON 1999/2000

Saturday, 20 November 1999: Munster 32 – Pontypridd 10

MUNSTER: M Mullins, J Kelly, K Keane, C Mahony, A Horgan, R O'Gara, P Stringer, P Clohessy, K Wood, J Hayes, M Galwey (capt.), J Langford, A Quinlan, A Foley, D Wallace.
Substitutions: J Staunton for Mahony (61), T Tierney for Stringer, M Horan for Clohessy (both 76), E Halvey for Foley, D O'Callaghan for Galwey (both 79).

PONTYPRIDD: B Davey, R Greenslade-Jones, J Colderly, J Bryant, G Wyatt, C Sweeney, P John (capt.), M Griffiths, F Vunipola, S Cronk, W James, I Gough, G Lewis, D McIntosh, R Parkes.
Substitutions: L Jarvis for Sweeney, J Lewis for Colderly, N Tau for Griffiths (all 48), M Lloyd for Lewis (70), R Sidoli for Parkes, G Williams for Vunipola (both 73).

Sunday, 28 November 1999: Saracens 34 – Munster 35

SARACENS: M Mapletoft, R Constable, J Thompson, K Sorrell, R Philby, T Lacroix, N Walshe, R Grau, G Chuter, J White, S Murray, D Grewcock, R Hill, T Diprose, F Pienaar (capt.).
Substitutions: K Chesney for Murray (55), D Flatman for Grau (60), P Wallace for White (63), P Ogilvie for Hill (65).

MUNSTER: J Staunton, J Kelly, K Keane, M Mullins, A Horgan, R O'Gara, P Stringer, P Clohessy, K Wood, J Hayes, M Galwey (capt.), J Langford, A Quinlan, A Foley, D Wallace.

Saturday, 11 December 1999: Colomiers 15 – Munster 31

COLOMIERS: JL Sadourney, M Biboulet, S Roque, J Sieurac, D Skrela, M Carre, F Culinat, JP Beyssen, M Dal Maso, P Pages, G Moro, JM Lorenzi, B De Giusti (capt.), S Peysson, P Tabacco.
Substitutions: B Lhande for Carre, JP Revallier for Lorenzi (both 61), N Marient for Moro (66), C Laurent for Dal Maso (80).

MUNSTER: J Staunton, J Kelly, M Mullins, J Holland, A Horgan, R O'Gara, P Stringer, M Horan, K Wood, J Hayes, M Galwey (capt.), J Langford, A Quinlan, A Foley, D Wallace.
Substitutions: I Murray for J Hayes (40), T Tierney for P Stringer, D Crotty for J Staunton (both 74), F Sheahan for Murray.

Saturday, 18 December 1999: Munster 23 – Colomiers 5

MUNSTER: J Staunton, J Kelly, M Mullins, J Holland, A Horgan, R O'Gara, P Stringer, M Horan, K Wood, J Hayes, M Galwey (capt.), J Langford, A Quinlan, A Foley, D Wallace.
Substitutions: J O'Neill for Horgan (28), D Crotty for Staunton (53), F Sheahan for Wood, T Tierney for Stringer (both 76), D O'Callaghan for Langford (79).

COLOMIERS: JL Sadourny, P Martinez, S Roque, J Sieurac, B Lhande, D Skrela, F Culinat, JP Beyssen, M Dal Maso, J Tomuli, JP Revallier, H Marient, F N'Tamack, B De Giusti (capt.), P Tabacco.
Substitutions: W Begane for Tomuli, G Moro for Revallier (both 40), P Magendie for N'Tamack, C Laurent for Dal Maso (both 60), P Pueyo for De Giusti (73).

Saturday, 8 January 2000: Munster 31 – Saracens 30

MUNSTER: D Crotty, J Kelly, M Mullins, J Holland, A Horgan, R O'Gara, P Stringer, P Clohessy, K Wood, J Hayes, M Galwey (capt.), J Langford, A Quinlan, A Foley, D Wallace.
Substitutions: T Tierney for Stringer (5-10), J O'Neill for O'Gara (11-16), M Horan for Hayes (15-22).

SARACENS: M Mapletoft, R Constable, J Thompson, K Sorrell, D O'Mahoney, T Lacroix, N Walshe, D Flatman, G Chuter, J White, S Murray, D Grewcock, R Hill, T Diprose, F Pienaar (capt.).
Substitutions: B Johnston for Thompson (21), P Wallace for White (60), M Cairns for Chuter (11-17).

Saturday, 15 January 2000: Pontypridd 38 – Munster 36

PONTYPRIDD: B Davey, G Wyatt, S Parker, J Bryant, R Greenslade-Jones, L Jarvis, P John, M Griffiths, A Lamerton, S Cronk, G Prosser, I Gough, GP Lewis, R Field, D McIntosh.
Substitutions: W James for Gough (50), J Colderley for Bryant (54), C Loader for Griffiths, M Lloyd for Field (both 62).

MUNSTER: D Crotty, J Kelly, M Mullins, J Holland, A Horgan, R O'Gara, P Stringer, P Clohessy, K Wood, J Hayes, M Galwey (capt.), J Langford, A Quinlan, A Foley, D Wallace.
Substitutions: E Halvey for Quinlan (50), M Horan for Hayes (69).

Saturday, 15 April 2000: Munster 27 – Stade Français 10

MUNSTER: D Crotty, J Kelly, M Mullins, K Keane, A Horgan, R O'Gara, P Stringer, P Clohessy, K Wood, J Hayes, M Galwey (capt.), J Langford, E Halvey, A Foley, D Wallace.
Substitutions: M Horan for Hayes (25 inj.), A Quinlan for Halvey (79), F Sheahan for Wood (30-35).

STADE FRANÇAIS: C Stoltz, C Dominici, F Comba, C Mytton, B Lima, D Dominguez, C Laussucq, S Marconnet, F Landreau, P De Villiers, P Auradou, K Whitley, D George, R Pool-Jones, T Lievremont (capt.).
Substitutions: R Froment for George (40), L Pedrosa for Landreau (67).

Saturday, 6 May 2000: Toulouse 25 – Munster 31

TOULOUSE: S Ougier, E N'Tamack, C Desbrosse, L Stensness, M Marfaing, A Penaud, J Cazalbou, C Califano, Y Bru, F Tournaire, F Belot (capt.), F Pelous, C Labit, S Dispagne, D Lacroix.
Substitutions: P Bondouy for Desbrosse (70), C Soulette for Califano (72), H Miorin for Dispagne (70), M Lievremont for Lacroix (65).

MUNSTER: D Crotty, J Kelly, M Mullins, J Holland, A Horgan, R O'Gara, P Stringer, P Clohessy, K Wood, J Hayes, M Galwey (capt.), J Langford, E Halvey, A Foley, D Wallace.
Substitutions: F Sheahan for Wood (40), D O'Callaghan for Galwey (78).

Saturday, 27 May 2000, in Twickenham: Northampton 9 – Munster 8

NORTHAMPTON: P Grayson, C Moir, A Bateman, M Atlen, B Cohen, A Hepher, D Malone, G Pagel, F Mendez, M Stewart, A Newman, T Rodber, D McKinnon, B Pountney, P Lam (capt.).
Substitutions: M Scelza for Stewart (67), J Philips for Newman (70), J Bramhall for Malone (73).

MUNSTER: D Crotty, J Kelly, M Mullins, J Holland, A Horgan, R O'Gara, P Stringer, P Clohessy, K Wood, J Hayes, M Galwey (capt.), J Langford, E Halvey, A Foley, D Wallace.
Substitutions: K Keane for Crotty (82).

SEASON 2000/2001

Saturday, 7 October 2000: Munster 26 – Newport 18

MUNSTER: D Crotty, J Kelly, M Mullins, J Holland, A Horgan, R O'Gara, P Stringer, P Clohessy, F Sheahan, J Hayes, M Galwey (capt.), J Langford, A Quinlan, A Foley, D Wallace.

NEWPORT: M Pini, M Mostyn, J Jones-Hughes, A Marinos, B Breeze, S Howarth, D Edwards, R Snow, J Richards, A Garvey, S Raiwalui, I Gough, P Buxton, G Teichmann (capt.), A Popham.
Substitutions: J Pritchard for Jones-Hughes (inj.), G Taylor for Raiwalui (22-25).

Saturday, 14 October 2000: Castres 29 – Munster 32

CASTRES: F Plisson, U Mola, E Artiguste, G Delmotte, P Garrigues, G Townsend, A Albouy, M Reggardo, R Vigneaux, L Tsabadize, S Chinarro, J Davidson (capt.), A Costes, I Lassissi, J Diaz.
Substitutions: A Larkin for Artiguste (33), F Laluque for Chinarro (46), G Bemaset for Tsabadize (50), C Batut for Vigneaux, D Dima for Reggardo (both 60).

MUNSTER: D Crotty, J Kelly, M Mullins, J Holland, A Horgan, R O'Gara, P Stringer, P Clohessy, F Sheahan, J Hayes, M Galwey (capt.), J Langford, A Quinlan, A Foley, D Wallace.

Saturday, 21 October 2000: Munster 31 – Bath 9

MUNSTER: D Crotty, J Kelly, M Mullins, J Holland, A Horgan, R O'Gara, P Stringer, P Clohessy, F Sheahan, J Hayes, M Galwey (capt.), J Langford, A Quinlan, A Foley, D Wallace.
Substitutions: K Keane for Mullins, J Staunton for Holland (both 77), M Horan for Clohessy, M O'Driscoll for Galwey, C McMahon for Wallace.

BATH: M Perry, I Balshaw, P de Glanville, M Tindall, K Maggs, J Preston, G Cooper, D Barnes, M Regan, C Horsman, M Haag, S Borthwick, A Gardiner, D Lyle, B Clarke (capt.).
Substitutions: A Adebayo for de Glanville (76), A Long for Gardiner (41-44).

Saturday, 28 October 2000: Bath 18 – Munster 5

BATH: M Perry, I Balshaw, P de Glanville, M Tindall, K Maggs, M Catt, G Cooper, D Barnes, M Regan, C Horsman, M Haag, S Borthwick, A Gardiner, D Lyle, B Clarke (capt.).
Substitutions: A Adebayo for de Glanville (76), A Long for Gardiner (41-44).

MUNSTER: D Crotty, J Kelly, M Mullins, J Holland, A Horgan, R O'Gara, P Stringer, P Clohessy, F Sheahan, J Hayes, M Galwey (capt.), J Langford, A Quinlan, A Foley, D Wallace.
Substitutions: M O'Driscoll for Galwey (27), K Keane for Kelly (73), C McMahon for Wallace (81), M Horan for Wallace (64-68).

Saturday, 13 January 2001: Newport 24 – Munster 39

NEWPORT: M Pini, M Mostyn, J Jones-Hughes, A Marinos, M Llewellyn, S Howarth, D Edwards, R Snow, J Richards, A Garvey, I Gough, S Raiwalui, A Popham, G Teichmann (capt.), J Forster.

MUNSTER: D Crotty, J O'Neill, K Keane, J Kelly, A Horgan, R O'Gara, P Stringer, P Clohessy, F Sheahan, J Hayes, M Galwey (capt.), J Langford, A Quinlan, A Foley, D Wallace.
Substitutions: M Mullins for K Keane (62).

Saturday, 20 January 2001: Munster 21 – Castres 11

MUNSTER: D Crotty, J Kelly, M Mullins, K Keane, A Horgan, R O'Gara, P Stringer, P Clohessy, F Sheahan, J Hayes, M Galwey (capt.), J Langford, A Quinlan, A Foley, D Wallace.
Substitutions: J Holland for Kelly (40), J Staunton for Crotty (72).

CASTRES: G Delmotte, F Plisson, O Sarramea, E Artiguste, P Garriguez, G Townsend, F Seguier, L Toussaint, R Ibanez, M Reggardo, F Laluque, J Davidson (capt.), J Diaz, G Taussaq, T Labrusse.
Substitutions: A Larkin for Plisson (67), A Albouy for Seguier (57), T Bourdet for Toussaint (55), S Bonorino for Reggardo (55).

Sunday, 28 January 2001: Munster 38 – Biarritz 29

MUNSTER: D Crotty, J Kelly, M Mullins, J Holland, A Horgan, R O'Gara, P Stringer, P Clohessy, F Sheahan, J Hayes, M Galwey (capt.), J Langford, A Quinlan, A Foley, D Wallace.

BIARRITZ: S Bonetti, P Bernat-Salles, P Bidabe, N Couttet, S Legg, F Botica, S Bonnett, E Menieu, JM Gonzalez, D Avril, JP Versailles, O Roumat, S Betsen, O Nauroy, C Milheres.
Substitutions: T Lievremont for Roumat (48), M Lefevre for Versailles (52), M Irazoqui for Milheres (64), M Lievremont for Betsen, B Daguerre for Couttet (both 70).

Saturday, 21 April 2001, in Lille: Stade Français 16 – Munster 15

STADE FRANÇAIS: C Dominici, T Lombard, C Mytton, F Comba, R Poulain, D Dominguez, M Williams, S Marconnet, F Landreau, P De Villiers, D Auradou, M James, C Moni, C Juillet (capt.), R Pool-Jones.
Substitutions: A Gomes for Juillet (73).

MUNSTER: D Crotty, J O'Neill, M Mullins, J Holland, A Horgan, R O'Gara, P Stringer, P Clohessy, F Sheahan, J Hayes, M Galwey (capt.), J Langford, D O'Callaghan, A Foley, D Wallace.
Substitutions: D O'Cuinneagain for O'Callaghan (70), M Horan for Clohessy (83).

The future is red: *Young players like Jeremy Staunton,
seen here in Munster's warm-up match against Wasps at
the start of the 2001/2002 season, ensure that the future
for Munster, and Ireland, is very bright indeed.*